D0392312

DATE

Publish Without Perishing

Publish Without Perishing
A Practical Handbook for Academic Authors

Peter Benjaminson

Reference & Resource Series

A Joint Project of the
National Education Association
and the National Writers Union

nea PROFESSIONAL LIBRARY
National Education Association
Washington, D.C.

Printing History
    First Printing: March 1992

Note

The opinions expressed in this publication should not be construed as representing the policy or position of the National Education Association. Materials published by the NEA Professional Library are intended to be discussion documents for educators who are concerned with specialized interests of the profession.

Library of Congress Cataloging-in-Publication Data

Benjaminson, Peter, 1945–
    Publish Without Perishing : A practical handbook for academic authors / Peter
Benjaminson.
        p.   cm. — (Reference & resource series)
    "A joint project of the National Education Association and the
    National Writers Union."
    Includes index.
    ISBN 0-8106-1544-4
    1. Scholarly publishing. 2. Learning and scholarship—Authorship.
3. College teachers as authors. 4. Authors and publishers.   I. National Education
Association of the United States.   II. National Writers Union (U.S.) III. Title. IV.
Series
    Z286.S37B46   1992
    070.5'94—dc20   [20]   91-45406
                                                                  CIP

To Annie and the three Susans

CONTENTS

FOREWORD

Publish or perish. Three words that describe the higher education imperative. Three words that foster immense frustration, or even strike terror, among college and university faculty.

The simple truth is this: the world of publishing, for the overwhelming majority of faculty members, is a strange and foreign land, complete with an unfamiliar language all its own and impenetrable rites of passage at every turn.

Publish Without Perishing is a guidebook to this strange and foreign land.

Peter Benjaminson is an experienced author. With three books to his credit, published by four different publishers. Benjaminson knows his way around book publishing. *Publish Without Perishing* directly confronts all the questions that trouble academic authors with manuscript in hand.

Benjaminson explains the book publishing process step-by-step and couples that with examples taken from the actual experiences—good and bad—of academic authors.

This book is the product of the collaborative efforts of two advocacy associations—National Education Association and the National Writers Union. The National Education Association has a long history as an effective representative for the interests of higher education. NEA publications reach over 100,000 higher education faculty, staff, and institutions. The National Writers Union, as Benjaminson notes in the text, has become the nation's most effective advocate for the rights of authors, both academic and trade.

We are pleased to offer you this practical handbook for academic authors. Enjoy.

REBECCA L. ROBBINS, Ph.D.
NEA Higher Education Publications

9

ACKNOWLEDGMENTS

Thanks to Timothy Crawford, Kim Fellner, Gordon Felton, Charlotte McGowan, Sam Pizzigati, Doug Powell, Lenore Robinson, Rebecca Robbins, Anne Wyville, and Karen Zauber at NEA and NWU for their patience and assistance; to Susan, Richard, Steven, Bob, John, Phil, Alex, Martha, Carol, Joan, and Sandra for their friendship and aid; to Ken Goldstein for his encouragement and support; to Bob Stein, Peter Skolnik, Virginia Barber, and Doe Coover for their work on "Sixteen Points to a Better Contract"; to Rachel Burd, Bob Claiborne, Marsha Cohen, Brooke Comer, Donna Demac, Alec Dubro, Andrea Eagan, Sara Friedman, Barbara Garson, Marvin Gettleman, Art Gatti, Karla Harby, Brett Harvey, Paul Hoeffel, Nora Lapin, David Lindorff, Dick Leonard, Leil Lowndes, Mary Lynn Maiscott, Phil Mattera, Bob Reiser, Cathy Revland, Ellen Schrecker, Jonathan Tasini, Kate Walter, and Paul Zuckerman for their work on "Sixteen Points" and/or their other union activities; to Thomas Adcock, Roslyn Bernstein, Jennie Buckner, Susan Cook, Fred and Jocelyn Jerome, Jack Krauskopf, Claudia Menza, John Oppedahl, John Polich, Susan Rossen, Ina Selden, Neal Shine, Bill Smith, Kim Sykes, Hiley Ward, and Steve Weinberg for their continued aid and friendship; and to Albert, Florence, and Annie Benjaminson and Susan Harrigan for their love, assistance, and understanding.

The Author

Peter Benjaminson taught investigative journalism and numerous other courses full-time from 1981 to 1991 at three major universities: the State University of New York at Binghamton, New York University, and Columbia University. He is the author of *Death in the Afternoon: America's Newspaper Giants Struggle for Survival* (Kansas City: Andrews, McMeel & Parker, 1984), which won the $10,000 Jim Andrews Communicator Award. He is also the author of *The Story of Motown* (New York: Grove Press, 1979). Mr. Benjaminson is the coauthor, with David Anderson, of *Investigative Reporting* (First Edition, Bloomington: Indiana University Press, 1976; Second Edition, Ames: Iowa State University Press, 1990.)

A former reporter for the *Atlanta Journal* and former reporter and bureau chief for the *Detroit Free Press*, Mr. Benjaminson later founded the Live Wire News Service. An active member of the New York Local of the National Writers Union, he is a graduate of the University of California, Berkeley; the Graduate School of Journalism at Columbia; and the Sloan Fellowship Program in Economics Journalism at Princeton. He is married to *New York Newsday* reporter Susan Harrigan. They have a ten-year-old daughter named Annie and a three-year-old Yorkie named Scarlett and live in Manhattan.

Chapter 1

IT DOESN'T HAVE TO BE THIS WAY

None but a blockhead ever wrote, except for money.
  —*Dr. Samuel Johnson*

Publish or perish.
  —*Faculty promotion and tenure policy at most of the nation's major universities*

America's academics, like bespectacled grains of wheat, are continuously ground between the millstones of two of the country's major intellectual industries: academia and publishing.

While continuing to teach, academics are required to publish more and more to retain their positions. As more of them are pressured to produce by an academic machine increasingly devoted to publishing and decreasingly devoted to teaching, more academics are propelled willy nilly toward the academic and commercial publishing industry.

Although many colleges and universities still give lip service to good teaching, all they truly care about is publication. In many departments at many universities, all tenure candidates are assumed to have good service and good teaching records: all that's ever seriously debated is their publication output.

As the race for publication increases in intensity, it becomes more and more difficult for academics to get their work successfully published, or, in many cases, to get work published at all. "The competition's incredible," historian Marie Tyler-McGraw has noted. "People in the social sciences have a hard time getting anything published, but publication is still tied to promotion and success."

To make matters worse, large mainstream trade presses now publish less serious nonfiction than ever before. And many university presses seek more trendy and less academic topics as

13

the mainstream nonfiction publishing business gradually seeps into their corner of the bog.

As a result of all this, commercial and university presses must fend off squadrons of desperate academics begging for publication, academics who are willing to give up many or all of their publishing rights to attain publication, or to actually pay for publication out of their own pockets.

And, as the market for serious books diminishes, the practices of academic and commercial presses are worsening. Some offer no advances, no royalties and no copyright protections for the author.

Susan Cavin, the assistant director of women's studies at Rutgers, wrote a book that was published in 1985. The first printing of the book sold out and demand was mounting for a second printing. Yet Cavin had received no royalties. The reason: her contract allowed the publisher to subtract many of the expenses of running his company from her royalties, even if the expenses weren't directly related to her book.

Beverly Guy-Sheftall's book, *Sturdy Black Bridges: Visions of Black Women in Literature,* was published by Doubleday in 1979 (Bettye Parker and Roseann Bell were the book's coeditors). "We never got any money for that book," Guy-Sheftall, an associate professor of English at Spelman College, says. "Our major motivation was to get the book out."

According to Professor Emeritus G. Thaddeus Jones of the Benjamin T. Rome School of Music at Catholic University in Washington, D.C., "Most young authors are happy to have their books published on whatever terms they can get, but often they undervalue their work." Jones didn't anticipate many sales of his second book, *Music Theory,* one of the Barnes & Noble College Outline Series, but he was wrong. It sold 5,000 copies a year for more than a decade.

Even for books that end up selling well, adequate editorial attention is rare. And most books suffer from insufficient promotion and go out of print with great rapidity. In

14

any case, both university and commercial book contracts usually favor the publisher. Sometimes contracts are not even offered.

B. J. Chandler teaches history at Texas A. & I. University in Kingsville. His first book was *The Feitosas and the Sertao dos Inhamuns: The History of a Family and a Community in Northeast Brazil from 1700–1930* (Gainesville: University of Florida Press, 1972. A Center for Latin American Studies Latin American Monograph).

"I never asked for or signed a contract," says Chandler. "None was ever given me. I wrote my doctoral thesis and the Center for Latin American Studies at Florida published it. There was no provision for royalties and no advance. I never made a penny, but I was grateful for getting it published."

John Elliott is a professor of theology and religious studies at the University of San Francisco. The university in Germany at which Elliott did his doctoral work insisted that the dissertations of all its doctoral candidates be published before the students would be awarded their doctorates.

"But my dissertation was a detailed academic work which I couldn't get a publisher to accept," says Elliott, who finally had his dissertation published "in a very prestigious series. It was an honor to be in it, but I haven't made one cent from it."

Academics often find themselves in a position in which they must accept such treatment.

"I felt I was going to be in for a pretty difficult tenure evaluation," says Robert Elias, an associate professor of politics at the University of San Francisco. Elias formerly taught at Tufts, which at that time was trying to become another Harvard. "The focus was pushed significantly in the direction of research, pushing teaching far down the line among the things you were evaluated for, for tenure. When you're in that position, it makes you less feisty."

When Oxford University Press offered Elias a book contract, "I thought 'Oxford is a reputable publisher and that's going to help me. I don't want to screw things up by debating with them. I'll just take the contract they offer and not argue with them.'"

Many academics know that some publishers take advantage of tenure-induced desperation, but many don't realize it doesn't have to be this way.

"Academics seem to speak just to each other. We live in a sort of isolated bubble as far as knowing what's going on in the outside world," says Faith Berry, an associate professor of English and comparative literature (teaching American literature and women's studies) at Florida Atlantic University. "As Granville Hicks once said, we are the timid profession."

Academics produce a significant portion of the books published in the United States, especially important nonfiction. In 1986, the 70 university presses produced more than one out of every 10 titles published, 3,500 titles in all. As this figure indicates, academic presses do a great deal of good. They publish books that wouldn't see the light of day otherwise and make those books available to thousands and thousands of people. Often they do it at a loss. Nevertheless, they still act a lot like, and are, businesses. The inexperienced should approach them with caution.

Yet academics often act like the callowest freshman among their students in their contacts with the publishing industry. Too often, academics accept substandard contracts, masking such acceptance with the rationale that their main source of income is from college salaries. Some professors, playing both ends against their own middle, claim they accept low college salaries because they have all those summers to write books and collect the royalties from them. Then they often accept low advances and royalties for the books they spend their summers writing.

But academic authors have just as much right to a substantial royalty income from their books as do nonacademic authors. Many academic books don't make money, but others do, and some textbooks are ranked among the most lucrative books of all time. Authors should be cut in more fully on the take

16

from their successful books, whether those books are published by university or commercial presses. And even where no substantial money is involved, academic authors are entitled to fair treatment. Numerous nonmonetary facets of book publication are as or more important to many academics than whatever money may be involved: keeping their books in print, for instance.

A book contract should be an academic author's bill of rights, not a catalogue of shame. But with the pressure that professors are under these days, it's often the latter.

"Most academics don't know anything about a book contract," said Berry. "They just sign one."

"Even if we find material that puzzles us in a contract," Elias said, "it's almost always explained away with 'don't worry about that' or 'this is the standard contract and we can't change that.' I got oral agreement on a few things that weren't in my contract. These things didn't fit within the boundaries of the standard contract and would have had to be added onto it. But if I had been confident enough and aggressive enough, I could have gotten better language."

What isn't in your contract isn't assured. David Walonick's second book, *Library of Subroutines for the IBM Personal Computer* (Glenview, Ill.: Scott Foresman, 1984), was scheduled "to be distributed with a disk; it was the only way it made sense," Walonick says. "But the publisher changed the plan midway. For some reason, without telling me, they published it without a disk. When I asked them why, I got a very abrupt answer, 'The decision was made to do that,' with no explanation given. But leaving off the disk made it a useless book. Buying it was like buying a user's manual without the software."

Pantheon published Howard Wachtel's book, *The Money Mandarins: The Making of a New Supranational Economic Order*, in 1986. Notes Wachtel: "They promised me they'd do a paperback edition orally, but not in writing, and never did one."

"Authors have mixed records with academic presses. A lot depends on your expectations," says author Paul Lipke. "How

17

much do you know going in? If you're wet behind the ears, you're in for a big surprise."

This book aims to eliminate that surprise. You *can* be a pro, publish successfully, avoid perishing, and maybe even get some money and satisfaction from your efforts. Many of our fellow academics have done all three. This book will give you information that will help you stiffen your spine when you approach publishers, even under tenure-track conditions, and help you get the most you can—in money and in satisfaction—out of the books you publish.

Included in these pages are the National Writers Union's "Sixteen Points to a Better Contract," the union's recommendations for concessions book authors should attempt to obtain from their publishers. Of course, you may not be able to extract many of these concessions from your publisher. But a contract is merely a publisher's first offer and you should consider it as such. It never hurts to ask for something. At the very least, asking shows that you're not undervaluing your work. At best, the publisher may concede several points merely because you asked him or her to do so.

Some publishing executives are equipped with several versions of a contract and are preauthorized to give the more pro-author versions to the authors who ask for concessions. And some publishers, although not terribly eager to change their standard contract, may consider your book of more worth than the cost of changing the clauses you question. In any case, what's important to individual authors may not necessarily be of any special importance to the publisher they happen to be dealing with at that moment.

"In my field," author Lipke says, "there are many amateurs who write on the side and don't get paid as much as they expected. Then they get bent up or hacked out of shape."

But hard words, raised voices, paranoia, and suspicion will get you nowhere and may well lose you your contract and any chance of dealing with that publisher in the future. Just ask for whatever you want politely and matter-of-factly. You may just get it. In any case, if you don't get the concessions on this book, you may get them on your next book, or your next book, or your next. You have a long professional career ahead of you.

Chapter 2

AGENTS: CAN'T LIVE WITH 'EM, CAN'T LIVE WITHOUT 'EM

> *Wombats sleep for up to twenty hours a day. I had an agent like that once.*
> —Host, *"Animal Crackups" TV Show, 1990*

> *Those who live upon the backs of artists—agents and entrepreneurs—are usually accorded a more prominent place in society than the originators of their wealth.*
> —Jon Manchip White discussing *Aztec society in* Cortes and the Downfall of the Aztec Empire *(New York: Carroll and Graf, 1989)*

Most academic authors don't have agents, since articles are what academic writers write most often. Although agents sometimes handle magazine and journal articles for clients who are also writing books for them, they rarely handle articles for anyone else.

This isn't to say that most academics who are writing a book couldn't use an agent. But in most cases they can't afford one. Comparatively small royalties and advances are the norm in academia, and agents make their living by taking a percentage of what their authors earn from writing. So academic authors, especially unknown academic authors, are unlikely to find an agent who'll handle their work. In fact, an unknown writer may find it more difficult to sign on with an agent than to obtain a book contract directly from a publisher.

Some argue that since academic authors are usually paid so little, they shouldn't give away a portion of their meager earnings to an agent. This argument ignores the practical reality that an agent—if you can get one—usually means a more lucrative contract for the author. So it behooves an author—academic or otherwise—to find one if at all possible.

Faith Berry's view of agents is somewhat jaundiced. "Most agents only want you when you're big enough so they don't have to do anything for you. They want a marketable product. They don't want to help you; they don't want to market you. They want a known commodity."

This isn't universally true. Some agents will spend a lot of time on new clients. Unfortunately, those usually aren't the agents with the most clout.

But having an agent saves loads of time. "I don't have to send out pitch letters, manuscripts, any of that crap," says author John Sandman (although he points out that agents won't necessarily handle everything their clients write, unless those clients are superstars.) If you really want to write, as opposed to wanting to be a famous author, you can leave negotiation and sales to your agent. You can also ask your agent rudimentary legal questions that you'd have to pay an attorney a relatively stiff hourly fee to answer. Agents also don't charge an hourly rate for the time they spend reassuring or consoling you. On the other hand, lawyers don't take a percentage of your writing income on the projects they handle for you.

FINDING AN AGENT

The best place to find the name of your future agent is in *Literary Market Place* (New York: R. R. Bowker, published annually) or *Writer's Market* (Cincinnati: Writer's Digest Books, published annually).

Check the "Author's Agent Subject Index" in *Writer's Market* for agents handling manuscripts in the subject area you're writing about. You'll find your agent's address and phone number, what sorts of works are handled, at what fee, some recent sales made by that agent, etc. You can find similar information in *Literary Market Place*. These annual directories are published and available late in the year *preceding* the year printed on their covers.

You should then call the local unit of the National Writers Union (NWU) (see Appendix A) to check your newly gathered information against the union's agent data base. The information in the data base is contributed by NWU members who deal with agents. The member indicates how many books the agent has sold for him or her, then ranks the agent on a scale of 1 to 5 for accessibility, persistence in selling the author's work, ability to solve disputes with the author's editor or publisher, effectiveness in making subsidiary sales, editing ability, skill in negotiating contracts, interest in the author's writing career, and the extent to which the agent involves the author in selling and negotiating strategies. Each writer also rates the agent as an agent for new writers, for experienced fiction writers, nonfiction writers, children's/young adult writers, screen/TV writers, and magazine writers. The writer then indicates the reason for leaving the agent, if indeed he or she has left, and sends the questionnaire to the keeper of the NWU data base at the appropriate local. The keeper then provides the information, with the writer's name removed, to NWU members free of charge, on request.

Doing research in *Literary Market Place, Writer's Market,* and the NWU agent data base may be tedious, but it's very necessary. Very few agents work with all sorts of books and all sorts of writers, and some have deservedly bad reputations. It makes sense to save yourself some time by pinpointing the agent you need. Of course, you can also land an agent through a referral from a friend who is one of the agent's clients. If you can't get information on an agent any other way, you might try asking the agent directly what books he or she has sold recently, who wrote them, and what publishers they were sold to. Then call up the authors named and ask how successful the agent was for them.

Many inexperienced writers consider signing with any agent at all a great coup. Sometimes it is. "I sent an agent a manuscript and he got a contract for me in three weeks," said

Jack Weatherford, an associate professor of anthropology at Macalester College. "He knew the right person to call."

This is not always the case. Incompetent agents, mediocre agents, troublesome agents, and downright crooked agents exist in literary agentry as they do in every other field. There are no qualifications for declaring yourself an agent, a publisher, or an author. Just announce you're one and hang out your shingle. As the old saw goes, "Thirty days ago I couldn't spell 'agent' and now I is one." Whether you know a book proposal from a marriage proposal is another question.

One way to avoid some incompetent or crooked agents is to obtain a list of agents who belong to the Society of Author's Representatives or the Independent Literary Agents Association, who must adhere to certain standards to be members. Not all honest and competent agents are members of these two groups, however.

The ideal agent is constantly in touch with publishers and cognizant of their current needs. After all, there are many good book ideas out there and many good publishers and authors; the problem is putting all three together during the same lifetime. Doing so is the agent's job, even if that means planting the idea to bring the match about.

I once ignored this theory and lost a chance at a big book contract. I had what I thought was a great book idea and took it to a New York agent. She didn't like my idea, and suggested a different one. Stupidly, I ignored her suggestion and went to another agent, who had the same reaction to my idea and the same suggestion for another project. I should have realized that the well-connected agents I was talking to didn't dream up their ideas in their sleep. The idea they were suggesting to me probably came from a publisher. Just a few weeks later, after I had made it clear I wouldn't write the suggested book, another author was signed to do it. A couple of years later, the book was a high-quality bestseller.

If you have a purely commercial idea for a book, an agent will help a lot. Large commercial publishing houses are much more likely to look at your book and much more likely to pay you a large advance if you're represented by an agent. Editors at many large publishing houses look only at book proposals submitted by agents. On the other hand, some academic and small presses are much more likely to deal directly with authors than with agents, partly because they know they'll have to pay less to an agentless author. According to Paul Parsons in his book *Getting Published: The Acquisition Process at University Presses* (Knoxville: University of Tennessee Press, 1989), fewer than four percent of manuscripts published by university presses in one recent year were brought to their attention by literary agents. Nevertheless, many commercial houses publish textbooks and trade books written by academics. The solution: send your proposal or manuscript to an agent first. If you make no headway with agents, find a publisher for your first book on your own, then make a second run at getting an agent. An agent will be much more likely to take on your book project if you've already interested a publisher, and you'll be spared a lot of unnecessary, nonauthorial contract negotiation in the bargain.

AGENTS WHO CHARGE FEES

Avoid the ripoff agents who charge authors for reading their work, and for reading the revised versions they suggest the authors write, and for reading the revised versions of those revised versions at so much per revision ad infinitum. Confusing this issue is that some big, successful agents run operations of this sort as a sideline. Scott Meredith, whose author/clients have included Norman Mailer, Judith Krantz, and James Clavell, charges $400 to read a "book script" up to 100,000 words, $500 for book scripts between 100,000 and 200,000 words, and up to $900 for book scripts over 300,000 words. However, if you've sold a book, screenplay, or teleplay to a *major* publisher or producer *in the past year*, no fee is charged. Writer Joe Queenan revealed in the *New Republic* that Meredith's minions seemed willing to read and comment at least somewhat favorably on any proposal accompanied by a check. Some so-called agents do only this; some legitimate agents, like Meredith, do this as a sideline; some other legitimate agents charge a reading fee, but tell you what they really think about the book even though they may never get another fee from you after you hear the truth; and some legitimate agents don't charge a reading fee at all. Know what the fee is before you agree to anything.

The National Writers Union urges all authors to avoid agents who charge fees. "They have no business charging fees," said an NWU official. "It's pure exploitation. By charging fees, they're subverting the original intent of agentry, which is that they're not supposed to get paid until you get paid. They're also muddying the water: their fee charging makes it difficult for writers to figure out what's legitimate and what's a scam."

Indeed, what's nice about agents who don't charge a reading fee is that they make money only when you make money. The standard rate for an agent at this writing is 15 percent. Some agents are trying to drum up business by taking only 10 percent. Others are charging 18 percent. Eighteen percent is almost as high as the usurious interest rates charged by major credit card companies; on the other hand, if the agent doesn't sell your book, you pay nothing. Some agents charge you directly for copying costs, telephone expenses, etc., they incur on your behalf as well as their percentage fee, although some of the agents will reimburse you for these fees when they sell your manuscript.

Sometimes this can get annoying. "I broke off with the agent I had when he went up to 18 percent,"said Weatherford. "The increase just didn't seem right. I already had to pay for the xeroxing he did on my behalf and the long-distance calls he made to me. He was charging each phone call to me, nickel and dimeing me to death. A $2.25 call would go on the statement at $2.25. If he'd just charged me a higher percentage from the beginning instead of adding on all those little charges I probably would have stayed with him."

Weatherford's next agent, Lois Wallace, charged 10 percent and paid for her own phone calls. Weatherford also liked the way she treated him face to face. "I sent her a copy of my first book with a letter of introduction. She liked the book and set up an appointment to see me the next time she was in town. She made me feel like the most important person in world. Just talked about me me me. I later realized she had a huge clientele—but she acted like she was just starting out and wanted to get people on her list. My former agent was always telling me about his other clients and how important they were. But I wasn't interested in that. I was interested in how can I do this? How can I do that?"

SIGNING A CONTRACT WITH YOUR AGENT

You may like your agent at first meeting, but it will be a while before you know how well you and your agent are going to get along or how he or she will do with your project. Sign a short agreement defining your relationship. If the agent doesn't offer you a contract, just write him or her a letter containing your understanding of your oral agreement. Don't sign an open-ended contract or a contract covering a specific number of years, just an agreement allowing the agent to represent you on one project. If things work out for both of you, you'll want to sign up for your next work as well. If things don't work out, once the agent has finished handling the one piece of work you brought in, you can gracefully say goodbye and take your next work to another agency.

Be certain to include in the agreement what percentage your agent will collect and whether or not the agent has an option on your future books. Don't insist on a contract before the agent looks at your work, but do sign one before the agent sends your work to editors. Written contracts are best: good fences make good neighbors, and good contracts make for good agent-author relationships.

A contract with your agent will make other agent-author situations easier to handle as well. For instance, an agent is handling one of your book proposals but you suspect he may have stopped sending it out. Rather then pester him with endless phone calls asking what he's doing with your proposal, send him a note asking him to save time for both of you by listing the editors or houses to whom he has sent the manuscript. His response will let you know whether or not he has indeed been sleeping on your job. If he has, and you have located someone else who might do better for you, you can at this point write the first agent a letter thanking him for his efforts on your behalf but letting him know that you're going to be seeking another agent. You can then provide the second agent with the information from the first agent, thus helping the second agent avoid the time-wasting faux pas of sending your proposal to the same houses to which the first agent had sent it.

Agents are not mere machines for handing off proposals to panting couriers from publishing houses, nor are they merely Geiger counters for sensing publishing trends. A good agent will take the time to carefully examine your proposal and/or manuscript to see if it can be improved for quick sale to an appropriate publisher. Why spend time and money sending out a proposal or manuscript that isn't perfect? If your agent keeps sending out a proposal that publishers keep rejecting, think about signing with another agent. Do the same if the agent only sends a proposal to a couple of houses, then tosses it in a file drawer; many major authors have been offered contracts on the fifth or sixth submission.

Agents of my acquaintance are deluged by unsolicited manuscripts from authors. They step over piles of unopened manuscript envelopes at the office; they find three-foot piles of unopened jiffy bags stuffed with manuscripts outside their apartments when they go home every night; truckloads of marked-up manuscripts pursue them in their sleep; boatloads of unread manuscripts follow them across the River Styx. So, you're asking yourself, why bother to send a manuscript to an agent? The answer: don't. Approach an agent the same way you'd approach a publisher—send a proposal, or a couple of chapters, or an outline and a couple of chapters. (See Chapter 4, Preparing Proposals.)

Chapter 3

COLLABORATION: DO YOU WANT TO DO IT ALONE, OR WITH SOMEONE ELSE?

By all means marry: if you get a good wife you'll become happy; if you get a bad one, you'll become a philosopher.

—*Socrates*

Writing is a lonely profession. The quiet room, the humming screen, the distant noises all conspire to isolate the writer. Such isolation can affect your work as well as your psyche: after an extended period of isolation, thoughts that may seem unimportant to others grow dangerously large in your brain. Each time they circulate through your isolated gray matter, they gain additional substance. Eventually, they may twist your work into a shape the healthy, convivial you would not even recognize.

Isolation drives many would-be writers into public relations, journalism, burger flipping, advanced schizophrenia, and . . . teaching. Teaching and writing are, in fact, a good combination, since the hours and the tenure system encourage—nay, require—writing, and the contact with students and other faculty members stimulates the flow of ideas. Nevertheless, writing itself is still lonely and possibly less fruitful than it would be . . . if you worked with a collaborator.

Problems definitely stem from collaboration, but so do several advantages:

1. Speed. You'll be able to write a book in half the time it takes your colleagues, who must sit alone in their offices and sculpt a solo manuscript into existence.

2. You don't have to beg a friend to read your first or second draft. Your collaborator will criticize your work enthusiastically. After all, your collaborator's

29

name will be on the book along with yours.

3. Your collaborator will quite likely be willing not only to critique but to rewrite your draft chapters and vice versa. At each stage, you'll each feel emotionally and intellectually superior to each other and your manuscript will get better and better.

4. You can bounce your ideas off your collaborator, who's quite likely to be saner about your ideas than you are about your own, and vice versa.

5. You can combine your technical expertise in one field or subfield with your collaborator's complementary expertise and not have to educate yourself in a whole new area in the process of writing your book.

6. In collaboration, two is greater than the sum of one plus one. The synergy involved in two author/experts thinking and writing about the same project may well produce a product greater than the sum of your individual qualifications and abilities.

Computers and modems have made collaborating much easier than it used to be, especially long-distance collaborating. Rather than sending bulky partial manuscripts through the mail, marking them up awkwardly in pencil, and putting them back in the mail again, latter-day collaborators can transmit their copy to each other's computers via their modems, edit it, and send it back with great speed and minimum fuss. (Most computers, no matter what make they are or what word-processing software they use, can exchange words and data through use of files saved in the standard computer interchange code called ASCII—pronounced "ask'-ee.")

Using computers for editing is not only speedier, it's easier on the ego: a change made by a computer doesn't look like a change. The manuscript looks as if it had always been written that way.

There are, of course, problems involved in collaboration.

1. You have to split the royalties. For most academic books, since royalties are penny ante and time is tenure, this may be much less of a worry than speed of production. And remember, if the book does become a big commercial success and you have royalties to worry about, at least you'll have someone to go on half the talk shows for you.

2. You may argue over exactly how you'll split the royalties. A fifty-fifty split is the obvious solution if you're each going to write half the book and then rewrite the other's half. If one coauthor is only going to write a chapter or two, you could arrange to give that coauthor a proportional percentage of the royalties. Any such arrangements between or among collaborators should be spelled out in writing either in your joint contract with the publisher, in a separate agreement between you, or in both documents. You should also include a clause in these documents guaranteeing each of you a percentage of the advance and royalties from the eventual book if either of you drops the other for a third writer.

3. You may argue over the nature or direction of the book, and split up. But at least you would have had the benefit of a stimulating argument and the partial manuscript you created together.

4. You may be insulted by remarks your coauthor lets fly in critiquing your part of the manuscript. Resist any thought of retaliation. As your mother used to say when spanking you with her hairbrush, it's for your own good.

5. You may argue over whose name comes first as author. If you're generous, you'll allow the person with the weakest tenure case to go first. On a later edition of the book, you can put your collaborator's name last to even things up. (Note *Investigative Reporting*, First Edition, by David Anderson and Peter Benjaminson

31

[Bloomington: Indiana University Press, 1976] and *Investigative Reporting*, Second Edition by Peter Benjaminson and David Anderson [Ames: Iowa State University Press, 1990].)

6. Coauthors may feel they did more than their partners. The solution: try to work with someone you worked with on another project, even a nonwriting project, a person whose work habits you know. You might also read that person's other work to determine if you'll each be contributing the same level of maturity to the manuscript.

7. Your tenure committee may look more askance at a coauthored book you submit than at a single-authored book. However, you might well be able to write two different books with two different coauthors during the period in which your fellow tenure candidates are struggling alone in their offices to write one book, thus impressing the tenure committee with your boundless productivity, especially if your name appears first on at least one of the books.

Academic coauthoring teams are often formed through contacts made at academic conferences. One of Arthur Quinn's colleagues at the University of California, Berkeley, made a significant discovery about the Bible and its relationship to earlier ancient Near Eastern myths. The colleague, Isaac Kikawada, had written a huge manuscript, but didn't know what to do with it. An editor at Abingdon Press was intrigued with the manuscript, but didn't know how it could be presented as a book of interest to anyone other than a handful of scholars. Quinn and Kikawada met on a conference panel and discovered they were working in the same direction. "He suggested I look at the manuscript and rethink it so it would appeal to a larger audience," Quinn says. (Quinn is a professor of rhetoric.) Their joint book *Before*

Abraham Was: The Unity of Genesis 1–11 (Nashville: Abingdon Press, 1985) proved successful.

Sometimes coauthorships arise from less formal propinquity. "I was in charge of a lot of teachers," notes Quinn, who at one point in his career trained instructors in argumentative writing. "I popped off one day about an idea I had for a textbook. One of the senior instructors, who had just finished her Ph.D. and didn't want to work on her dissertation anymore, suggested we work out the idea together." They did, and a new book was born.

Chapter 4

PREPARING PROPOSALS

*Old freelancers never die; they just send out their
final book proposal.*

—Anonymous

Academic authors seem to spend half their lives writing their books. Years in the library are followed by decades at the word processor. Summer, fall, winter, and spring fly by. Finally, the manuscript is ready. The academic sends it off. The editor who receives it takes one look at the bulky, uninviting bundle of pages and throws it in the corner. There it sits. Forever.

One way to avoid this fate is to know someone at the publishing company, or someone who knows someone at the publishing company, who will make sure your manuscript is read and considered.

But you may know no one at the appropriate company or you may know no one at all in publishing. Your best bet, then, may be to send out a proposal, or a proposal and sample chapters, rather than the bulky manuscript, even if you have finished the manuscript. Editors are human. Given much to read, they'll read the shorter items first. (Note: Some editors insist on an outline and sample chapters; some prefer a proposal letter; others want the complete manuscript. Check in *Writer's Market* for your target editor's preference or write, enclosing a SASE [a self-addressed stamped envelope] for the publisher's guidelines.)

Writing and sending a proposal **before** completing the manuscript is an even more efficient method of selling your book. After all:

1. Why write a book if no one will publish it? It probably won't help your tenure case and won't help you much otherwise. You can find out if someone will publish

your book by sending out a proposal before you spend the years necessary to write a complete manuscript.

2. Editors like to participate in the formation of a book. By sending the editor a proposal rather than a manuscript, you make it possible for editors to get a word in edgewise about how to structure the book before you complete it. This isn't a surrender of academic freedom; you don't always have to take the editor's advice. But you at least ought to consider that advice, especially if a few organizational rather than substantive changes will make the difference between your masterwork remaining in your desk drawer or being distributed by helicopter to wildly cheering crowds.

3. The more suggestions an editor makes about the book you outline in your proposal, the more forcefully the editor will argue for it at meetings of the editorial board that decides which proposals or manuscripts to accept. So by doing less work at the beginning, you may be rewarded with a larger payoff later on.

4. This may border on heresy to some authors, but there's always a chance your editor's pre-manuscript suggestions may help you improve the book. If you send the editor a proposal rather than a manuscript, the editor is more likely to give you those suggestions, because all editors know it's easier to amend a partially written book than a fully written book. And you'll be the beneficiary. Rather than tearing hundreds of pages into little bitty pieces, you'll be able to write them right in the first place.

5. Even if publishers reject your initial proposal, you can send them the manuscript when you're through with it. Arthur Quinn took this route, writing many of the same houses that had rejected one of his and a coauthor's book proposals. "You weren't so interested last time, but now we've finished the manuscript," he

wrote them. "For obvious reasons you couldn't envision how it was going to turn out, but now you can see what we did with the idea."

These comments about book proposals apply to fiction as well as nonfiction. Editors don't have much time to read, period; when it's a complete manuscript you've sent an editor, it doesn't matter whether it's fiction or nonfiction: it may still go to the bottom of the pile. And even fiction editors like to participate in the formulation of the book and come up with useful ideas pertaining to the manuscript. Send out a brief description or overview of the book plus sample chapters and make both your life and the editor's much easier.

Even if the press to which you send your proposal demands to see the completed manuscript before considering your book further, you can then send it to that press with confidence that they're interested enough to take a look at it. When you send a manuscript out without sending a proposal first, you have no idea whether a publisher is interested in plowing through your manuscript or not.

Sending out a proposal instead of a completed book narrows the gap between conception and sale and makes book writing a lot more fun. When Quinn and coauthor Nancy Bradbury sent out their book proposal, "We explained why we were dissatisfied with the similar books then existing. We then explained how we would structure our book, provided a sample table of contents, and explained how we would write each chapter. We sent the proposal to a few houses and soon had four presses interested. We were used to going hat in hand; it was great to have publishers competing for us." Macmillan published their book, *Audiences and Intentions: A Book of Arguments*, in fall 1990.

Writing a good proposal isn't easy. The proposal should be as well written as the manuscript itself, even though it won't be published. In fact, the proposal should be written better than the manuscript; if the proposal's no good, no one will ever read your manuscript, except in Xerox or samizdat.

A book proposal should, in essence, say what your proposed book is about, who you are, why you're qualified to write it, what the competition is, if any, and what the audience would be. All this information is of major interest to a potential publisher. Moreover, gathering and analyzing this information in writing may compel you to reassess your own book idea and either improve it or drop it entirely.

A proposal should rarely be much longer than six double-spaced typewritten or computer-printed pages. The shorter your proposal is, the better. It can be accompanied by an outline of the entire book plus a sample chapter or two. To save yourself postage and copying costs and to save the editor unnecessary reading time, you might want to send the proposal per se first, with an offer to send the outline and sample chapters at the editor's request.

Remember to include a SASE with your proposal. This may seem a small point but try to imagine yourself an editor with 50 proposals piled in a corner. Which would you reply to first—those proposals that came with stamped self-addressed envelopes or those without?

Don't overpromise. On the other hand, don't write your proposal with palsied hands, shaking with fear that you'll be held to every jot, tittle, and promissory note in it. Once you actually write more of the book than the sample chapters, its structure, tone, and organization may well change and the finished product may be quite different from the proposed and outlined product. Editors know this and will not require you to reproduce every nuance in your proposal in your finished work. (If your plan for writing the book changes significantly, though, you might want to let the editor know, but the editor's most likely response will be to tell you to do what you think best.)

Think of your proposal more as a sales document than a work of literature. The proposal has only one purpose: selling your book idea. If it sells your idea, it's a success. If it doesn't, it's a failure. Don't imitate a noisy TV commercial, but do think sale.

One beneficial task the proposal will force you to undertake, if you haven't previously done so, is to go to the library and bookstore and look up competing works. If you're teaching in the field, you're familiar with many competing works, but only an hour or two in the library or store will acquaint you with all of them. It's embarrassing when a publisher asks you how your proposed book will differ from Book X and you have to think fast to cover up the fact that you've never heard of Book X. Better that you know about Book X and have designed yours to fill a gap Book X doesn't fill.

When listing the competing books, include all relevant material, including the publisher, the author, and the book's exact contents. Don't be afraid to provide your opinions of each book, without becoming emotional. Make it clear what your book would do that other books haven't, or note the changes in the field that have made the competing books irrelevant and yours relevant. If the competing book or books are out of print, make that clear in your proposal also. The *Subject Guide to Books in Print* (New York: R. R. Bowker, published annually) is a big help here.

If you're lucky, as I've been, there will be no other competing books on the market when you are pitching a book proposal in a particular field. David Anderson and I sold the proposal for *Investigative Reporting* (Bloomington: Indiana University Press, 1976) at a time when no textbook on investigative reporting had ever been written, during a massive upsurge of interest in the field inspired by Watergate. I sold the proposal for my second book, *The Story of Motown* (New York: Grove Press, 1979), at a time when no other book about the Motown Record Company had ever been published (although a thesis-like book about Motown's music had been published in 1972). I sold the proposal for my third book, *Death in the Afternoon: America's Newspaper Giants Struggle for Survival* (Kansas City: Andrews, McMeel and Parker, 1984) at a time when no one had published a book about the death of big-city afternoon and evening newspapers in the United States. Selling book ideas is relatively easy when there's no competition.

In your proposal, be as specific as possible about your potential audience. It does no good to claim that every literate person will be interested in what you're writing about; that's never the case. Although the larger the potential audience the better, you will do yourself and your editor more of a service by pinpointing the exact groups that would be most interested in your proposed book, including the organized groups or associations of which they might be members. The idea: to show there's not only a large audience for your book but an audience that's easily reachable at meetings and conventions, or through mailing lists. In fact, the editor may make your proposal the basis of the marketing plan for your book. You should also indicate, if it's not already clear from the context, why these people would buy your book.

Include a proposed title for your book but make it clear you know the title is tentative. Editors decide titles; authors object to them, usually too late and without success.

If you have already written about the subject of your book in journals or periodicals, you might want to include copies of those articles with your proposal to indicate your expertise and your qualifications as a writer. Do not send originals of any articles and do not send unpublished articles, but do send relevant well-written clips. You should mention any teaching and/or professional experience that makes you an expert in the field, any previous books you've done and any rave reviews your books have received.

If you're trying to sell a book as a trade book (a book that will be sold in bookstores to the general public) as opposed to an academic book or a textbook, you might want to emphasize any connections you have with magazine editors or talk-show hosts that will help you get parts of the book serialized or publicized.

When Anderson and I proposed *Investigative Reporting* to a number of publishing houses simultaneously, we used the two-stage proposal technique mentioned above: a proposal followed, only if requested, by an outline and sample chapter. The proposal read:

Dear Mr. Smith:

A colleague and I have completed a first draft of a book on investigative reporting techniques. We have shown key chapters to a number of other investigative reporters and journalism instructors and their response has been enthusiastic. [Get on the bandwagon.]

According to the Library of Congress [authoritative source] no other books have been published on this very important topic, although volumes abound on journalistic subfields such as feature writing and political reporting. [No competition but much interest.]

We believe our book will be of immense appeal to journalism students and novice journalists who aspire to investigative reporting, as well as to working reporters, investigators for citizen and consumer groups, and that segment of the general public interested in what goes on behind the headlines. [Fairly specific audience delineation.]

[Qualifications] I am an investigative reporter for the Detroit Free Press. I am also City-County Bureau Chief for that newspaper and an adjunct professor of journalism at Wayne State University in Detroit. I also have worked as a correspondent for the Washington Post and Newsweek magazine and as a reporter for the Los Angeles Times and other California newspapers.

My associate, David Anderson, worked for the City News Bureau in Chicago, the Lerner Newspapers chain, and the Associated Press. He is currently a reporter at the Free Press. He was associate editor of the Chicago Journalism Review and has won a number of awards for his investigative reporting.

Mr. Anderson was a fellow at the University of Chicago Urban Journalism Program, where he began research on the book. I attended the American Press Institute's Seminar for Investigative Reporters, where I gathered complementary material.

If you are interested in our manuscript, we would appreciate hearing from you at your earliest convenience.

Sincerely,

Those publishers expressing an interest in the manuscript received this second letter and the enclosures specified:

Dear Ms. Johnson:

Enclosed please find five draft chapters of the book on investigative reporting techniques referred to in your assistant's letter of May 28. The chapters are entitled: The Man in the Snap-Brim Fedora; Public Records; Election Fraud and Election Records; Approaching and Interviewing Sources; Summing up the Story; and Confronting the Principal.

Other chapters deal with choosing subjects to investigate, evaluating tips, planning the investigation, the preliminary decision to investigate, and the art of the brief investigation.

We also have written a second chapter on public records, a chapter on nonpublic records, and others on dropping an unsupportable investigation, writing the investigative story, getting the story past the editors, following up the story, the use of gadgetry, mistakes to avoid, and ethical problems encountered by investigative reporters.

The chapters we have not sent you are now being read and criticized by other investigative reporters at other newspapers.

Throughout the book we have sought not only to pass on information but also to convey some of the work-related attitudes of good investigators. To this end, the manuscript will include reprinted investigations illustrating a number of techniques discussed in the book. Each investigative story will be accompanied by comments by its author.

Because we feel our book is so timely and should be published as soon as possible to take advantage of the present widespread interest in investigative journalism, we have sent copies of the enclosed chapters to other publishers who have asked to see them. We hope this doesn't inconvenience you.

If you are interested in seeing our other chapters or in discussing publication arrangements, please let us know. Thank you for your consideration.

Sincerely,

Indiana University Press bought our book proposal and kept the book in print for 11 years. We then sold the second edition to Iowa State University Press, which published it in 1990.

Proposals vary in format. When Robert Elias was trying to sell his first book, *Victims of the System: Crime Victims and Compensation in American Politics and Criminal Justice* (New Brunswick: Transaction Books, 1983), he sent out a two-page description of the book, a chapter or two, and a table of contents including a description of what he proposed to do in the remaining chapters.

For his second book, *The Politics of Victimization: Victims, Victimology, and Human Rights* (New York: Oxford University Press, 1986), Elias sent out an outline, a description of what he was going to do in each chapter, a sample first chapter, and a marketing analysis to about 40 publishers.

Sara Evans, who teaches history at the University of Minnesota, was trying to sell her first book, eventually published as *Personal Politics: The Roots of Women's Liberation in the Civil Rights Movement and the New Left* (New York: Knopf, distributed by Random House, 1979). She sent an outline of her dissertation and two 20-page papers she'd delivered, instead of a formal proposal, to "a whole bunch of publishers."

"I had an attack of arrogance," Evans says. "I just thought I was working on something important. Some of the publishers said they didn't look at unsolicited manuscripts, and some said they didn't look at dissertations, but two or three said,

'It looks very interesting and we'll be happy to look at it when it's done.'"

Showing your proposal to someone other than yourself before sending it out would be a wise move. Many less-experienced writers are loath to show their work to anyone. They spout various excuses for not doing so, some grounded in superstition, but their true motivation is fear of criticism. Force yourself to seek such criticism rather than hide from it; better your proposal be revised before an editor sees it.

Choose your target publishers by looking up the subject you're writing about in the Book Publishers Subject Index of *Writer's Market* or in Appendix B of this book, looking at your favorite books published in your field, examining the promotional literature publishers send you, listening to colleagues who have been published at particular houses, or talking to editors at academic gatherings. *Writer's Market* lists the names and addresses of editors at each publishing house who receive unsolicited proposals. *Writer's Market* also indicates whether that house accepts unsolicited proposals (or manuscripts) and in which fields. Even though *Writer's Market* is usually accurate and is published annually, take the time to call your target publishing house yourself and find out if the editor listed in *Writer's Market* remains the appropriate target, or, for that matter, if that editor remains in that house's employ. Mobility is endemic in publishing, as elsewhere.

It always makes sense to find out not only what press specializes in your area but what press is aggressively soliciting manuscripts. B. J. Chandler of Texas A&I University was trying to sell the manuscript that later became his book *The Bandit King: Lampiao of Brazil* (College Station: Texas A&M University Press, 1978).

"A mentor of mine in Florida tried to make contacts for me with both Columbia and Oxford, but nothing worked out," Chandler says. "So I began to look for places I thought were more realistic. The University of Texas seemed a more logical place. A friend of mine there urged me to submit my manuscript but said it might be a year or a year and a half before I got a decision on acceptance. He suggested Texas A&M, which had a lot of money; the director of the University of Texas Press had moved to A&M and was building up the press there. I got a 'yes' in six weeks."

Since writers often complain that their publishers fail to adequately publicize their books, it makes sense to send your proposals to those presses that do the best jobs of publicizing books in your field. Bill Robinson of Iowa State sent the manuscript of what became his first book, *Brains & People: An Essay on Mentality and its Causal Conditions* (Philadelphia: Temple University Press, 1988) to Reidel, in the Netherlands, because "I was getting their advertisements for books in the mail. They were aggressively circulating their wares."

The publisher liked Robinson's manuscript, but only one of the publisher's two readers did. So Robinson sent his manuscript to Temple University Press, because, he said, Temple regularly advertises in the programs of meetings of the American Philosophical Association, and by direct mail. Temple published it.

Having an in with a publisher, even through a coauthor, always helps. David McCurdy, a professor of anthropology at Macalester College, published for years with coauthor James P. Spradley. At one point, Spradley had published a book with Little, Brown, and McCurdy and Spradley wanted to sell Little, Brown a book they had jointly edited.

"We wrote a prospectus, then approached a Little, Brown editor at a national meeting," McCurdy says. "Spradley's book had been successful and our book sounded like a good idea to them. We gave them a three-page prospectus. I don't think they had it reviewed; they just jumped on it."

The book became *Conformity and Conflict: Readings in Cultural Anthropology*, edited by Spradley and McCurdy (Boston: Little, Brown, 1971).

By the time McCurdy and Spradley were ready to publish their next book, an editor from Science Research Associates who was going to start a series in McCurdy's field had visited him, and McCurdy was able to talk him into publishing his next book as part of that series. It became *The Cultural Experience: Ethnography in Complex Society* (Chicago: Science Research Associates, 1972).

For a later book, an introductory textbook in cultural anthropology, McCurdy and Spradley sent out prospectuses to Little, Brown, John Wiley and Co., and one other publisher. McCurdy and his coauthor then "campaigned" this prospectus, handing it out at a national meeting of anthropologists. They finally sold it to a John Wiley editor they met at a national meeting, and it became *Anthropology: The Cultural Perspective* (New York: John Wiley and Co., 1980).

You may be an academic, and you may be publishing mainly for prestige and tenure, but why not try for some big bucks along the way? If your book is on a popular subject, send it to the major publishing houses and to agents who handle commercial books before you send it to editors at university presses. If a commercial press takes the book, you score (although if you don't have tenure, getting your book published with a major commercial press might make you a victim of faculty jealousy and eventually cost you tenure, unless the book is seen as sufficiently academic). Even if commercial houses don't buy your proposal, they might, through expressing their doubts about it, show you ways to improve the proposal before you send it on to other houses either commercial or academic.

You may say that few academic subjects are likely to be published by commercial houses. Yet recent hardcover bestsellers include *The Closing of the American Mind*, by Allan Bloom (New York: Simon & Schuster, 1987), *The Rise and Fall of the Great Powers: Economic Change and Military Conflict from 1500 to 2000*, by Paul Kennedy (New York: Random House, 1987), *The Man Who Mistook His Wife for a Hat and Other Clinical Tales*, by Oliver Sacks (New York: Summit Books, 1985), *The Name of the Rose*, by Umberto Eco (San Diego: Harcourt Brace Jovanovich, 1983), and other books that a few years ago would have been found only in the furthest reaches of the darkest library. The growth of illiteracy and the popularity of television have obscured a parallel movement in American culture: the vast increase since World War Two in the number of college-educated Americans hungry for meaty books to devour.

SIMULTANEOUS SUBMISSION

Many successful publishing scenarios are heavily influenced by chance: a proposal or manuscript arrives when an editor is thinking about publishing a book on the subject and a deal is swiftly made. On the other hand, sometimes a proposal arrives just a week or so too late. Long periods of time, often a year or more, routinely elapse between the submission of a book manuscript and its acceptance or rejection. The solution: simultaneous submission. Although many university presses won't stand for it, it's worth a try. According to Paul Parsons in *Getting Published*, a recent survey of university press policy on simultaneous submissions showed that 37 percent of university presses accept simultaneous submissions, and 52 percent typically refuse them but make exceptions. Only 11 percent refuse simultaneous submissions on all occasions.

There's nothing ethically wrong with submitting a proposal to several publishers simultaneously as long as you tell them in your cover letter that you are doing so. Sending a proposal rather than a full manuscript is an advantage here since editors receiving a proposal submitted simultaneously are more likely to read it than a simultaneously submitted manuscript. Even if editors refuse to consider a simultaneously submitted proposal, they may still give you a key bit of information, such as that they have decided to no longer publish books in that area. Knowing this early on will save you a great deal of time, time you may be able to spare early in the tenure process but time you won't be able to spare after you finish the manuscript, much later in the tenure process. Since tenure decisions sometimes depend on a publisher's acceptance of a book on a Thursday instead of a

Friday, such a gain may be crucial for your academic career. Even if a publisher does publish in your area, but refuses to consider your proposal or manuscript because you submitted it elsewhere simultaneously, you may have whetted an editor's interest in the topic. When you send it back on an exclusive basis, that editor may well be eager to look at it. There's almost no way simultaneous submission can backfire.

Although author Robert Elias complained about his acceptance rate when sending out simultaneous submissions—"I didn't have a very good batting average. I sent it out to thirty places and got positive responses from six"—he then had six positive responses to choose from.

With publishers as unpredictable as they are, sending your proposal to as many as possible is one of the keys to successful freelancing, academic or otherwise. Elias described the reaction to one of his proposals as "bizarre . . . The places I thought I had a really good chance with returned it. It didn't seem they'd even read it. Other publishers I thought too good or the subject matter not even up their alley responded."

Eventually, and such is every author's dream, the publishers will come to you. When Robinson finished his first book, he said, he vowed he "wouldn't write another book ever, or at least for ten years. But the editor at Temple took me out to dinner to convince me to write another one." Since Robinson actually had another book idea in mind, he finally decided to ignore his vow and get busy.

But before you begin work on your second book, you have to get your first book accepted. Some editors get annoyed if you pester them with queries about a manuscript or proposal you submitted, but sometimes it's better to risk their annoyance than to lose track of your manuscript. Marie Tyler-McGraw says the University of Georgia misplaced her manuscript on the history of the colonization movement in Virginia and did nothing with it for a year after asking her to send it in.

"Then they didn't say anything until I called," she said. "I could have sent it to other presses in the meantime. If I had known then what I know now, I would have bugged them after three months."

Tyler-McGraw read the university's three-line apology for the mishap as a rejection letter, "since nothing in it indicated they were interested." She asked that the manuscript be sent back to her, and some would say this was Tyler-McGraw's second mistake. She should have capitalized on whatever guilt Georgia felt at losing the manuscript—if indeed, that is what happened—by forgiving the press politely and urging the editor to go ahead and read her manuscript.

COVER LETTER

If you insist on sending a university press your unsolicited manuscript rather than a proposal, at least put a good face on what you're doing by sending a decent cover letter with the manuscript.

Never address the cover letter to "Dear Editor." What's your reaction to a letter that arrives at your office labeled "Dear Professor"? Call the press and get the name of the editor to whom it would be appropriate to mail the manuscript.

Indicate in your cover letter that you know something about the press and its publishing program. Mention other books in your field that that press has published and where you think your manuscript would fit in. As in a proposal, write about why the press should publish your book and state specifically what your book is about and your qualifications to write it.

REJECTION

Rejection is a tricky business. When Arthur Quinn first began approaching presses, he used to take rejection letters at their face value.

"Time and again you get these rejections saying it was an absolutely wonderful manuscript and we all loved it, but it just didn't fit into our list," Quinn says. "But after you get a sufficient number of these, you realize it's just a convenient way to brush you off. They don't want to get into a shouting match with you about how good your manuscript is. Their rejection letter is generic. What they're actually doing is cutting things off as cleanly as they can. If I'd been aware of that early on it would have saved me lots of grief."

Some publishers and publications make it as easy on the rejected author as possible. One Chinese magazine sends out rejection letters that read: "Thank you for sending us your wonderful and thought-provoking article. It was, in fact, too good for our humble magazine. Although we strive diligently, we believe ourselves totally unworthy of printing such a magnificent piece of scholarship."

Book publisher Thunder's Mouth Press of New York takes a different approach: its response to some submissions is a postcard bearing a picture of a skunk accompanied by the words, "Your manuscript gave us heartburn. Have you ever thought of needlepoint?"

The only healthy response to rejection slips of any sort is the stunt pilot approach. When stunt pilots crash—assuming they are relatively uninjured—they are sent right up again so they don't lose their nerve. When academic authors get rejections, they should immediately send out their proposals again, so *they* don't lose their nerve. This technique is easier on the spirit than sulking, since once you've sent your proposal out again, you're once again waiting for a response rather than sitting forlornly with the evidence of defeat staring you in the face. In any case, the sooner you send out the proposal again, the sooner it will be published, and the sooner you'll be able to satisfy the tenure committee.

Many academics have encountered a variegated sort of rejection, the sort that Arthur Quinn experienced: their work is neither clearly academic nor clearly popular.

"Leonard Nathan and I wrote a short introduction to the work of Czeslaw Milosz—the Pole who won the Nobel Prize in literature in 1980," Quinn says. "We both had had a long, warm friendship with him. After he won the prize, Nate and I thought most of what was interesting in Milosz' work was being missed or ignored by American critics and that a 100-page book would help American readers figure him out. But the commercial houses said this guy wasn't as important as Johnny Carson and Danielle Steele, and the academic presses said the book was too simple: they wanted Slavic scholars writing eruditely about him."

The two authors were just about to give up when Nathan noticed that a new editor had been appointed at Harvard University Press. Although Harvard already had rejected the proposed book, Nathan sent it back there, and the new editor accepted it. The book, *Czeslaw Milosz: An Introduction to His Work*, was published by Harvard in 1991. Remember, giving up is non-professorial.

Sometimes, however, things work out initially just the way the author wants them to. Quinn sent a proposal and three sample chapters for his second book, which he described as "an attempt to see the whole of world history in a single place," to a number of commercial and academic presses. Then he sent it to a couple of small presses. One sent him a positive response, so he sent the complete manuscript.

"That publisher, with breathtaking rapidity, phoned and said he hoped I hadn't given it to someone else," says Quinn. "It happened the way I dreamt it would happen." The manuscript became *Broken Shore: A Perspective on History* (Salt Lake City: Peregrine Smith, 1981).

Chapter 5

PEER REVIEW: A LONG WALK ON A SHORT ONE?

Between the author . . . and the public . . . stands the shadow.
— *With apologies to T.S. Eliot*

An editor who finds your manuscript or proposal interesting enough to consider will typically send it out to one or more readers: people with expertise in your field who can provide the press with what is supposed to be an objective scholarly opinion on the worth of your manuscript. Unfortunately, most fields are divided into two or more factions, and a manuscript can be killed by a reader who's a member of the opposing faction or merely an enemy of yours. Also, since readers are paid as little as $75 to read what is often a full-length manuscript, and are often quite busy, they may give your manuscript a cursory reading or let it sit on their desk for months.

This can be a real problem if you're up for tenure or for reappointment and need something read, accepted, and published quickly. Karen Brodkin Sacks' book, *Sisters and Wives: The Past and Future of Sexual Equality* (Westport: Greenwood, 1978) was published in hardcover by Greenwood, but Sacks, the director of the Women's Studies program at the University of California, Los Angeles, would have preferred the University of Illinois Press since it had better distribution in women's studies and in labor at the time.

"Illinois was interested in it," says Sacks. "But it took them forever to get the reader's report. I was on tenure track and needed to stay on it, so I went with Greenwood." Illinois published the paperback edition of the book in 1982.

A dearth of outside readers can also cause a press to publish your book much later than is healthy for sales. A publisher asked John Elliott to write a manuscript in nine months. The publisher then sat on it for a year and a half and published it about six months later than planned.

"The problem was that the editorial board was unfamiliar with the commentary I was writing and they had few outside readers," Elliott says.

Readers can be used to advance corporate as opposed to the author's interests. Howard Wachtel signed a contract with a major publisher in 1979 to write a textbook in labor economics. He spent several years writing chapters.

"They kept sending the chapters out to different readers at each stage," says Wachtel. "Then I'd rewrite them and they'd send them out again. They sent them out to an equal number of readers who they knew would and knew wouldn't like the book. They said they had to neutralize a potentially antagonistic constituency. But as I told them, the way the field was divided there were certain people who would never approve of the book's approach. Sending the chapters to readers in both camps allowed them to make a corporate decision [to kill the book]."

Once you're told your manuscript is being sent out to reviewers, you might want to ask politely how many—and how long the reviewers are being given. Such information will at least prevent you from panicking unnecessarily as the months wear on. You might also want to ask if your editor is aware of the different factions within your discipline and if this knowledge has been taken into account in choosing the readers to whom to send your manuscript. This is important, since reader reports count heavily when an academic publisher's editorial committee, which usually consists of faculty members from the press' campus and press administrators, makes the final decision on which manuscripts to publish.

Chapter 6

ADVANCES: IT'S WHAT'S UP FRONT THAT COUNTS

The advance should be at least as much as the cost
of the lunch at which it was discussed.
—Calvin Trillin

Yes, advances do exist, even in academia. For most academic books, advances range from $1,000-$10,000. For many academics, and for many outside academia, $1,000 is important on its own. In the form of an advance, it's also important for other reasons:

1. If something goes wrong and your book is not published, the larger your advance, the larger the consolation prize: the advance itself. If you're struggling for tenure, the fact that you received an advance may help you with the tenure committee. In some departments at some universities, the larger the advance, the more the help. At the least, a large advance will pay some of your moving costs if your enemies on the tenure committee triumph.

2. Even if nothing goes wrong, relatively few authors receive more than the advance as payment for their work on the book. The contract may call for royalties, but the royalty threshold may be so high it may never be attained. So when you think of an advance, think of it as the total monetary compensation for all the work you put into the book.

3. The larger your advance, the more the publisher has invested in you, and the more likely the publisher is to protect its investment by publicizing and distributing your book. And if the publisher doesn't publicize or distribute your book very well, once again you'll have

your advance to fall back on. You won't be forced to depend on the royalties the publisher is failing to garner for you.

A publisher gave David McCurdy and his coauthor an advance of approximately $3,000 each and a $5,000 grant to spend on development costs for a book they contracted to write in the early 1970s.

"That was a lot of money then," McCurdy notes. "We hired a student researcher and each bought books and a typewriter. The more you can get them to invest in you, the more attention they'll pay to you because they don't want to lose their investment."

Jack Weatherford got a $7,500 advance for his first book, *Tribes on the Hill* (New York: Rawson, Wade, 1981).

"It was my first contract and I would have been happy with anything," says Weatherford, but $7,500 was a lot more than "anything," especially in 1979, when Weatherford received it. He was paid part of the advance on signing and part on turning in the final manuscript only a few months later.

If you submit your book to several publishers simultaneously, and are lucky enough to receive more than one offer to publish, there's no reason you shouldn't place your book with the publisher offering the largest advance, all else being equal. Of course, all else may not be equal. One publisher may guarantee quick publication, which you may need for tenure, while another is vague about the publication date but offers you an extra $200. The merits of each side in this sort of choice should be obvious. But there may be further subtleties, ranging from whether the higher-bidding publisher demands your copyright (see Chapter 9) to whether the lower-bidding publisher offers you a couple of extra weeks to read galley proofs. Which of these packages you choose will depend on your individual needs, or what you anticipate they may be at the time of publication.

Your calculations should also depend on what the word "advance" means to your publisher and when part or all of it will be paid to you. Be certain you and the publisher agree on the definition of the word "advance" before you sign your contract. Will it be paid to you in full when you sign the contract? Will it be paid one-third on signing, one-third on delivery of the first half of the manuscript, and one-third on delivery of the remainder of the manuscript? One-third on signing, one-third on delivery, and one-third on publication? Half on signing and half on delivery? Various percentages on signing, on evidence of completion of the first quarter of the work required to produce a completed manuscript, on delivery of the first half of the manuscript, on delivery of the completed manuscript, on completion of the editorial revisions, or on acceptance of the final draft? On publication only, which might be months away, or never?

Authors can control when their manuscript arrives at the publishers, but unless they own the publishing company, authors cannot order the presses to roll. Authors should therefore try to avoid tying their advances or any of their other rights as authors to publication. Your contract should contain words to the effect that, "The publisher agrees to print, publish, and distribute the book to retail and wholesale book sellers no more than 12 (18) months after receipt of the completed manuscript. If the publisher fails to do so, the author may request that this agreement be terminated. The publisher will then have sixty days in which to remedy the situation. If it is not remedied, all rights to the book will return to the author and the author will retain all monies already paid." This is as close to a must clause for a book contract as any. Leave this clause out and a publisher, through change of management or change of ownership or for some other reason, may bury your book alive. Leaving it out ignores the essence of a book contract: that the publisher agrees to publish your book.

The thought of a large or even a moderate advance may excite you, but remember that advances are advances on royalties (and not necessarily advances in the sense that they are paid to you either in advance of your writing of the book or the publisher's publication of it). Once you receive the advance, you won't receive another penny for your work until your royalties exceed the amount of the advance. To put it another way, your advance is subtracted from your royalties.

This philosophy guided Arthur Quinn and Nancy Bradbury when they were trying to choose between publishers for the book they were writing, *Audiences and Intentions.* The two publishers who wanted their book "were terrific and eager and enthusiastic and understood what we were doing," Quinn says. "In the end it was hard to choose between them. It was pretty clear that both could pay higher advances, but we didn't want to keep playing one off against the other. The money would come back in royalties anyway, and we liked the people and didn't want to lead them on."

But keep in mind that no one, repeat, no one, knows how many copies any book will sell and that the publisher can unintentionally keep sales low by failing to promote it, failing to send copies to the bookstore until a year after the reviews come out, or whatever. So the more you get in advance, the less risk you take that your net will come up empty.

The best possible world for the author would be one in which the entire advance would be paid on the signing of the contract. This is a goal rarely achieved by academic or other authors, however. A more realistic goal to fight for would be one-half the advance on signing the contract, one-fourth on delivery of half the manuscript, and one-fourth on delivery and acceptance of the full manuscript. This formula provides more of the advance near the beginning than the end, because the bulk of your work, such as research, is done nearer the beginning of your project.

A snake lives and hisses in the Garden of Eden of glorious advances, however: the refundable advance. The way many book contracts are written these days, if you fail to deliver the book, or if you haven't made a good faith effort to write a decent book, the publisher can ask you to return the advance. More alarmingly, many book contracts are written so that the publisher is free to say, when you've finished your 780-page tome, that your manuscript is unacceptable and your advance must be returned, even if you have made a good faith effort to write a decent book and have delivered it on time.

Now there may be many reasons for such an outcome. Your dog died, your enemies in the department denied you tenure although your fifty-sixth book was just published and your fourth multimillion-dollar grant just rolled in, and you learned that the holding company that owns your publishing house makes poison gas for use in orphanages. This caused you to lose your enthusiasm for the project, and you turned in a wretched piece of writing. Or perhaps you became a peyote enthusiast between stints at the word processor and decided, without informing your publisher, that you'd write a book about Mexican sunsets rather than the book on Wilhelm Reich's sex life you were contracted to write. In both of these cases, you should return the advance money.

Edwin Meese signed a book contract in 1988 that included a deadline of May, 1989 for delivery of his memoirs as attorney general. In June, 1989 he told a reporter he had already completed "a thousand pages." Yet he failed to deliver a single page by April, 1990 and the publisher rightfully cancelled his contract.

You're taking a similar risk of nonacceptance if you violate a provision of the contract by, say, turning in your manuscript after the deadline, or not turning in a manuscript of the length specified in the contract. If the publisher wants the book, he or she will forgive a violation of this sort and merely urge you to complete the manuscript, according to specifications, by a new deadline. If the publisher does not want the book, he or she may take this opportunity to void your agreement.

Although not completing the work may not be your fault at all, your publisher may still hit you up for the advance. After author James Baldwin died in 1987, McGraw-Hill sued his family to recover the $200,000 advance the company had paid him for his proposed memoir on the civil rights movement. The suit could have led to the eviction of Baldwin's 89-year-old mother from her New York home. This was one of the few suits ever filed against a dead author; suits against living authors are a lot more common, although few academic advances are worth the legal costs involved in such a suit. (McGraw-Hill finally dropped the suit, on the grounds that it was distressing the Baldwin family.)

An allegedly unacceptable manuscript might well be the publisher's fault. Perhaps the publisher didn't make clear what sort of manuscript was wanted. Perhaps the publisher decided, after signing the contract, that the book idea purchased from you wasn't as good as originally thought. Perhaps the publisher just lost interest in the project because the editors who were enthusiastic about your book are no longer with the company.

There's also the chance your publishing company will have changed hands by the time your completed manuscript is due. The new publisher may refuse to make a payment on a book the new managers didn't personally contract for. When Howard Wachtel gave his publisher the 400 pages of reprinted material and 200 original pages that constituted one of his manuscripts, the publishers, who had recently completed such an ownership change, said they "were no longer interested" in his manuscript (and refused to pay him the half of his advance they still owed him). "They didn't even bother to say the manuscript was unacceptable," Wachtel says. "I was young and naive and going through a divorce at the time so I didn't start a big hassle about their not following the contract." He should have.

"We thought we had a contract to publish a book," says another academic author, who asked that he not be identified. "The publisher had a habit of signing a lot of people to do books, then deciding when each book came in whether to publish it or not. They were buying fishing rights, not books. They would start making suggestions for changes here and there in chapters already turned in; then they would decide they were not interested in the project so they'd bail out. They strung along people for years that way.

60

"We brought it up with them that by this time, according to the contract, they were a little bit late with the next installment of our advance," continues this author. "They said, 'We hate to tell you this but the book won't go.' They spent a few thousand dollars just to have us in the bag legally if they liked the manuscript."

Publishers cannot be forced to publish a book against their will. At the same time they cannot expect to recoup the money they have advanced when they reject a manuscript that has been prepared according to the publisher's original direction. Authors who have fulfilled their obligations under the contract by delivering a manuscript are entitled to keep the advance even if the publisher decides not to publish the work.

Be sure you do fulfill your obligations under the contract. One way to do this is to give yourself a lot of leeway when filling in the blanks in the book contract. Someone in publishing once advised authors attempting to determine a delivery date for their manuscript to think deeply and carefully about all the tasks they will have to perform, add in extra time for all conceivable mishaps, and then multiply the total time by six. Very few people do this. If they did, few books would be written. But every writer should keep this formula in mind. Agree only to a realistic deadline. Release no manuscript before its time.

If during the writing of the manuscript you find yourself falling behind, arrange with the publisher for an extension of the deadline and get the extension in writing. It's said that publishers expect authors to miss deadlines, since everyone's an optimist when it comes to one's own writing. But an author who has missed a deadline is at the publisher's mercy, and if the publisher is new, unscrupulous, hard-hearted, hard-pressed, or merely under the gun, mercy may not flood forth just when you need it. In fact, it may be distinctly strained.

You also might try to insert a two- or three-sentence description of your book in your contract, or attach to the contract a copy of your book proposal, initialed by both you and

61

the publisher, so that the publisher will have a harder time denouncing your book as unacceptable.

Try also to insert language in your contract that calls for your manuscript to be "professionally competent and fit for publication" rather than "acceptable for publication." "Professionally competent" is a much more objective standard for outside observers, arbitrators, or mediators.

Although arbitration and legal action are always available as options, your goal as an author and an academic should be publication, not a long drawn out legal battle followed by a dinky settlement check sent to you at your new job in the refuse room of a major glue factory. You should, therefore, try to include the following clause, or something like it, in your contract:

> Unless the author requests otherwise, the editor shall make periodic review of the work and shall provide the author with written requests for specific changes. At the author's request, the editor will meet with the author to discuss the suggested changes.

This language will make it more difficult for your publisher to say that the completed manuscript was a complete surprise to him. But more importantly, it will tend to keep you in communication with your editor so that as the work develops you don't waste time writing something the editor is later going to remove from the manuscript, or writing an entire manuscript the editor will want to discard.

For the same reasons, try to include as much of the following language in your contract as possible:

> If the publisher finds that the author's final manuscript is not, in style and content, professionally competent and fit for publication, the publisher must, within sixty days of receipt of the manuscript, give the author a written statement outlining the respects in which the publisher feels the manuscript is inadequate. The author shall then have ninety days to submit changes to the manuscript.

Such language will, once again, give you a chance to communicate with the editor, discover what sort of material the editor wants you to write instead of the material you've already written, and then write it. Ninety days may not sound like much time, but if you can arrange the dates in your contract so that most or all of those ninety days are during the summer, a sabbatical, or a semester in which your course load has been lightened, you'll be able to utilize this relatively short period more productively.

All this assumes, of course, that any disagreements you have with your editor are disagreements over organization or writing style rather than principle. If your publisher wants you to write something you disagree with in principle, you'll have to decide whether getting your book published is worth loosening your moral fiber, or whether some compromise can be made which will accomplish the one without the other.

After you've spent ninety days attempting to make your manuscript acceptable to the publisher, it may be that your publisher will still find it unacceptable. Your final goal should be to block the publisher from not only refusing to publish your book but, in essence, charging you for the refusal. Try to get the following language into your contract:

Should the publisher maintain that the revised manuscript is still not professionally competent and fit for publication, the publisher may terminate this agreement with the following provisions:

a. All rights revert to the author
b. All materials and manuscripts shall be returned to the author
c. All advances paid to the author shall be kept by the author.

The chances that you'll be able to convince a publisher to include the language in Paragraph c in your contract, or anything like it, are minimal. However, no reason not to give it the old college try.

If your first publisher rejects Paragraph c and insists on repayment of the advance, suggest that your second publisher—once you find one—repay your first publisher. You can assure this outcome if you include in your contract wording to the effect that:

> Monies paid to the writer shall be repaid to the publisher out of the first proceeds from resale of the manuscript.

(This clause, called a "first proceeds clause," is an excellent fallback substitute for Paragraph c.) In realspeak, this means your second advance will go directly to your first publisher. Not as good as keeping the first advance and then getting a second advance from the second publisher, but better than a poke in the eye with a sharp stick. Beware, however, of what has been called the "false first proceeds clause," which makes you liable for repayment of your first advance out of your own pocket unless you repay from first proceeds (i.e., your second advance) *within the year*. You might be able to beat this deadline or you might not, but why put yourself in that sort of bind?

In any case, remain optimistic about reselling your manuscript. You already sold the manuscript to one publisher, so you may well be able to sell it to another, one more in agreement with the way you've written it. And this time, of course, you'll have the manuscript written. If you had more than one expression of interest when you first circulated your manuscript or proposal, the targets for your second sales offensive should be obvious.

Chapter 7

ROYALTIES: THE KING AND QUEENMAKERS

> *Some of his authors, however, did not praise Mr. Knopf so highly, for he disliked paying big advances and his royalty arrangements were said to be modest. "My God!" he once said of an author who pleaded for a sizable advance. "This man tells me he needs money to pay his grocery bills. What the devil do I care about his grocery bills?"*
> —From New York Times *obituary for Alfred A. Knopf*

Royalties are like reverse income taxes. When it comes to paying taxes, the more you make, the higher a percentage you pay. When it comes to royalties, the more copies of your book your publisher sells, the higher a percentage of the price of each book returns to you as royalties.

And, like taxes, royalties usually are arranged in brackets. The standard royalty rate offered by both commercial and academic presses for hardcover books is 10 percent on the first 5,000 books, 12$^1/_2$ percent on the next 5,000, and 15 percent thereafter, and 5 or 6 percent for each paperback sold.

But as in many other aspects of life, and of book publishing, the reality is all over the map. Commercial royalties vary and royalties in academic publishing vary even more. The royalties you should be paid will be written into your contract. Ask for changes in your royalty structure if you find that structure unpalatable.

Aside from differences between the royalties paid on hardcover and soft cover books, different royalties are also paid on books sold abroad. And some university presses will pay no royalties whatsoever on scholarly monographs that are not expected to make any money for the press involved.

There are also different prices the royalty rate can be applied to. Make certain that your royalties are calculated on the list price of your book (the cover price of the book minus a three or four percent "freight charge") not on the "publisher's receipts," a very flexible term.

For B. J. Chandler's second book, *The Bandit King: Lampiao of Brazil* (College Station: Texas A&M University Press, 1978), he signed what he considered a standard university press contract. Although it provided for no advance, he says, it did provide for 10 percent royalties on the first 2,000 copies sold, 15 percent on the next 3000, and 20 percent on all copies sold above 5,000.

However, these percentages were percentages of the publisher's receipts. Chandler would have been much better off had his royalties been calculated on the list price of the book.

Publishers normally sell books to bookstores and distributors at a discount of 49 percent or less. Although the publisher receives much less than the full retail price, your royalties, expressed in percentages, are still based on that price. However, under the terms of many book contracts, on "special sales" (often to organizations), if the publisher sells your book at a discount of 51 percent or more, your royalty will be based on what *the publisher* receives, not the cover price of the book. This means that if a book you wrote that carries a 10% royalty rate and $10 cover price is wholesaled at $5.10, your royalty is $1. If it's discounted to $4.90, your royalty drops to 49 cents.

To protect yourself, try to insert some of the following language in your contract:

On all books sold through normal trade channels, the writer shall receive 100 percent of the normal royalty based on the cover price of the book.

On books sold by the publisher outside regular trade channels at a discount of greater than 50 percent but less than 61 percent, the writer shall receive two thirds of his or her regular royalty; on those discounted more than 60 percent but less than 71 percent, one half the regular royalty.

Royalty rates often vary on mail-ordered books as well. Citing the cost of filling mail-order ads, publishers insist that on books sold by mail, which usually bring the publisher almost the full retail price, the author should receive only one-half the normal royalty. Worse yet, when a contract allows a publisher to make royalty calculations on mail-ordered books on the basis of the publisher's receipts rather than the list price of the book, you could wind up with a $1^1/2$ percent royalty on a book that is supposed to bring you 6–10 percent. Try to modify this clause if at all possible.

Faith Berry pointed out that while some authors get 10 percent royalty rates, "big name authors get 20 percent. One academic publisher offered me 6 percent, and I refused it. You only get what you demand."

Some academic authors suffer grievously in the royalty department. B. J. Chandler's first book was his University of Florida dissertation, which Florida published. He received no royalties and no advance.

John Elliott received almost as raw a deal. His book *1 Peter: Estrangement and Community* (Chicago: Franciscan Herald Press, 1979) was published by the Franciscans, a religious order pledged to poverty. "Anybody who publishes with them apparently has to pledge themselves to poverty also," says Elliott. The Franciscans gave him $100 for the manuscript. No royalties were to accrue to Elliott until after 3,000 copies of the booklet had been sold. But, says Elliott, the publisher does absolutely no advertising, making the 3,000-copy threshold unlikely to be attained. Also, since the booklet sells for $1 or $1.50, the royalties Elliot might receive would hardly be substantial. Elliott knew all this, of course, when he made the arrangements with the Franciscans, but "I wanted to make a contribution to the series of which the booklet was a part—a small paperback series for layfolks studying the bible—so I didn't concern myself with the finances of it." And Elliott, who is an ordained Lutheran clergyman as well as an academic, saw his writing, in part, as a contribution to the church. "You have some ideas you want to get out," says Elliott, "and that's more important than how much people will pay for them." Nevertheless . . .

Some academic authors, although they receive an advance and royalties, settle for lower royalties than subsequent experience indicates they would have been justified in receiving.

"I was satisfied with my contract at the time because I didn't know any better," says one academic who asked not to be identified. "But I'm not really satisfied with it now. I've broached the subject of higher royalties to my publisher," but as yet he has made no headway.

"You have to negotiate a hard contract at the beginning; you have to know the worth of something," this author says.

But the same academic points out that "If I were to go to my publisher with a second book, the success of the first book would be a good talking point. I would have some reason to know that it would sell well; they'd know I'd know what I was talking about." This is true of anyone who continues to write books in one field: with each book the author has a better base for negotiation.

ROYALTY STATEMENTS

Royalties can be tricky. But royalty statements are even trickier. "I get royalty statements," Robert Elias said. "But they're written in Chinese. I have no idea what they mean. They don't provide a running tally [of book sales]. They give you a count for the period but it's hard to figure out what that period is."

Complete and understandable royalty statements will help you make certain you are getting the royalties owed you.

For instance, it's helpful to know not only how many books were sold, but how many were printed, bound, and shipped. If the publisher printed, bound, and shipped 20,000 books and you receive royalties for 10,000 sold, you can, rightfully, ask where the missing 10,000 books are.

Royalty statements should include full information on the number of copies printed, bound, sold, returned, and given away during the period of the royalty statement, as well as the number of copies in stock at the end of the royalty period.

The statements should also include a clear accounting of the numbers of books sold in each price category, the royalty percent owed per book sold and returned in that category, and the total amount of money owed per category. They should also include a full accounting of money earned through other sources: foreign sales, sales of subsidiary rights, and so forth. (See Chapter 11.)

A bewildering royalty statement doesn't automatically mean your publisher is hiding something. But it may well mean part of his organization is not operating up to par, and complaints from authors might inspire reforms.

Under some book contracts, the publisher can deduct "royalty overpayments" on one book from your earnings on your next book from the same publisher. That is, if your royalties aren't large enough to repay your advance on your current book, the publisher can take the unrepaid amount due out of the earnings from your next book. Watch out for and object to any contractual arrangement of this sort. It could cost you.

So could another innocent-looking contractual blip. Many publishers claim the right to hold back a certain percentage of your royalties for six months, on the assumption that booksellers will return some books unsold. This claim is advanced most frequently with paperbacks.

You may feel you have to agree to such a clause in order to obtain your contract. But try to keep the percentage of held-back royalties at 25 percent or less and try to ensure that the publisher holds your money no longer than one royalty period, usually six months.

Chapter 8

SUBVENTIONS: YOU DON'T PAY, YOU DON'T PLAY

Publishing is like prostitution. First, you do it for love. Then you do it for a few friends. Then you do it for money.

—With apologies to Baudelaire

After you've come up with the idea for your book, sold the idea, researched the book, written it, rewritten it, revised it, compiled the index, obtained the permissions, and read the proofs, you may have to perform one more task: convince your university or a foundation to contribute a few thousand dollars toward your book's publication, or, possibly, pay such an amount yourself.

In commercial publishing, several major vanity presses compete for business from authors who are willing to pay the entire cost of producing the books they've written. It's these companies who are responsible for the "Authors sought by New York publisher" and similar ads that appear regularly in many magazines.

While such companies print the books their authors pay them to print, they may be even weaker on the publicity and distribution front than more traditional publishers. In April 1990, a Manhattan jury awarded a total of $3.5 million in damages to 2,200 Vantage Press authors after the authors complained that Vantage, the largest vanity press in the country, had duped them into believing their books would be placed in bookstores and advertised to the general public.

University presses as well as vanity presses often require monetary subsidies on behalf of their authors. At least eight university presses indicated in *Writer's Market 1990* that they engage in subsidy publishing. Princeton University Press

71

indicated it subsidy publishes 30 percent of its books, the University of Calgary Press indicated it subsidy publishes all of its books, the University of Illinois Press 30 percent, the University of Minnesota Press only translations, the University of Tennessee Press 10 percent. Most of the presses that indicate they engage in subsidy publishing also indicate they do not ask authors themselves for subsidies, but Princeton University Press, the University of Minnesota Press, and the University Press of Virginia, for instance, indicate they are not above accepting a subsidy from an author.

A 1983 survey by Columbia University Press editors quoted by Paul Parsons in *Getting Published* revealed that 49 percent of the 70 responding English and romance language departments at selected universities said that their institutions "occasionally" provided subsidies to support publication of books by members of their faculties. Another 7 percent "frequently" did so.

Some presses say they need subvention money to publish books with very limited audiences and/or high production costs. They point out that orders from libraries and other professors for many scholarly books are half what they were a few years ago, due mostly to budget cutting and high book prices. And they argue that the authors will be repaid for their efforts in helping to raise subvention money, or in paying it, in the form of promotions, raises, and tenure.

Some presses say that the availability of a subsidy has no effect on whether the book will be published or not. But other presses say some books won't be published unless an outside subsidy is received. A major problem with all this is that it's those in most need of publication—the untenured—who are least likely to be successful in convincing their universities to contribute such subsidies.

Colleagues told B. J. Chandler, he said, that they had been asked for subventions of $6,000–$8,000 by well-known university presses. "If I had spent five years researching and writing a book and were faced with the possibility of not publishing it at all or giving a subvention to a respectable university press—not a vanity press—I'd consider it," says Chandler. "And assistant professors, who don't have tenure and whose tenure might depend on getting a book published, are over a barrel."

The reason so many subventions are kept secret, Chandler adds, is that "subsidy publishing has a very bad name. It implies the press will publish anything you pay them to publish. And this feeling spills over onto university presses that accept subsidies."

"Paying a subvention is akin to vanity publishing," Faith Berry says. "You do it just to be published, just to have a book on your resume."

John Elliott paid E. J. Brill $1,000 in the mid-1960s to publish his first book, *The Elect and the Holy* (Leiden: E.J. Brill, 1966). Elliott pointed out that not only did he have to pay, but Brill charged so much for each copy of the book that few readers could afford it. It's now out of print.

Arthur Quinn had a similar experience with his first book, *The Confidence of British Philosophers: An Essay in Historical Narrative* (Leiden: E. J. Brill, 1977). "I was in a situation of publish or perish and had a manuscript that was going to annoy analytic philosophers. I got a favorable response initially from Knopf, then sent the book to the University of California Press, and got one positive, one favorable review and was axed, so I sent it to Brill. The contract required me to personally subvent $4,000–$5,000 of the publishing cost. Much of that came back in time, I think. It was that or be out of work. It was all right as long as it was a good series that had high standards. If it had been a vanity press, I wouldn't have done it."

Even if someone else pays your subvention, disadvantages remain. The Concordia Seminary in St. Louis, where Elliott was teaching, provided him with subvention funds from its graduate program for the publication of *The Elect and the Holy*. Elliott said that as part of this arrangement, Concordia, not Elliott, became the legal copyright holder. Elliott has been having trouble getting his copyright back ever since. (See Chapter 9.)

Since authors already subsidize the publishing industry through their willingness to accept low advances and royalties, asking them to serve as fundraisers for, or fund payers to, some of those same publishers is a bad joke. Only our counterproductive tenure system, which requires frantic efforts to publish on one side of the tenure wall, and no efforts whatsoever toward publication on the other side, would inspire such requests.

Academic authors should make as much use as possible of the academic grapevine, directories such as *Writer's Market*, and Appendix B of this book to find out which presses are interested in which field or subfield so that the author's query or manuscript is directed to a press that is enthusiastic about it and won't request a subvention. Authors should use the same grapevine and directories to avoid any contact with a press that demands subventions, even semi-routinely. And they should demand change in a tenure process that requires publication at any cost by a certain date on the calendar.

Chapter 9

COPYRIGHT (RIGHT) AND WORK FOR HIRE (WRONG)

> *[LeRoi Jones, later Amiri Baraka] went to lunch one day with a man from United Artists [for whom Jones was writing liner notes for record albums]. Talking terms, Jones said he wanted to be paid on receipt of the material (instead of the usual lengthy delay). "Oh, do you need money?" said the surprised executive.*
> —*From* How I Became Hettie Jones, *by Hettie Jones (New York: E. P. Dutton, 1990)*

What academic authors write is the authors' property, unless they sell it or give it away. This would seem naught but a simple statement of fact were it not that so many academic authors are willing to give their copyright to the first publisher who smiles in their direction.

Copyright gives you the right to do anything you want with your work, including the right to distribute and to reprint it. You can't legally throw your unpublished manuscript through your publisher's bedroom window or use it to start a fire in your agent's office, but you can copy it, sell it, print it, novelize it, and pocket the money from doing so, or have all the control you want over the people who do.

Under the most recent version of the United States Copyright Law, enacted in 1978, authors hold the copyright to their work as soon as they finish writing it. Under the previous copyright law, you had to register your copyright with the U.S. Copyright office before it became effective. You still may register your copyright, but even if you don't, the copyright is yours as soon as you finish your project.

Even though the law no longer requires it, it's a good idea to register your copyright as soon as possible after you've completed your project. Most inexperienced authors are scared to death that someone will steal their work, i.e., infringe their copyright by, perhaps, printing their work without payment and under the thief's name. That happens quite rarely.

Nevertheless, if your work is stolen, your first impulse will be to kill the thief. Let that feeling pass; it's nonproductive. Your next thought will be to sue the thief and to do so it will help if you have already registered your copyright. If you registered your copyright before your work was stolen, the law allows you to ask for much higher damages than if you hadn't done so. So register your copyright as soon as possible after you've completed the work.

To register your unpublished work, request an application form from the Register of Copyrights, Copyright Office, Library of Congress, Washington, D.C. 20559. Fill out the form and send it to the Register of Copyrights along with a copy of your work and $20, and your copyright will be registered. You can register numerous manuscripts of yours for the same $20 and with the same application if you send them to the copyright office under the same title, such as "Manuscripts by Jane Doe."

The copyright protection you register for will be in effect from the date of creation of the work until 50 years after your death. (This extra 50 years may seem superfluous until you remember that your estate will survive you and that many little John and Jane Does may be dependent on it.) If you wrote with a collaborator, your work will be protected for 50 years after the death of the longest-lived of you.

Whether or not you register your copyright, you're free to put the "©" symbol, followed by the year, and your name, at the top of your manuscript. Some say doing so makes you look like (a) an amateur, since your ability to write these words and the copyright symbol at the top of the page doesn't affect your copyright in the work or (b) an ignoramus who is unsure or unaware of your rights and likely to demand little in the way of money and fair treatment for your work. I think not doing so makes you look like (c) a wimp, afraid to stake your claim to what is rightly yours. Put the copyright notice at the top of your manuscript. Incidentally, you don't even have to be a high-tech author to show you know your rights: a pen and ink rendition of "©" is as acceptable as a four-color computerized day-glo three-dimensional reproduction of same.

Even if you mean to keep the copyright, watch out that your book contract doesn't steal it from you without your knowing it. Despite the new copyright law, which holds that in most cases writers own their copyright unless they reassign it, some courts have made exceptions and have granted copyright rights to the publisher. Strive to have the following clause inserted in your contract:

> The publisher agrees to publish a copyright notice in the book and to register a copyright in the author's name.

Another cautionary note: ideas, fact, and titles are noncopyrightable. The form in which you write your idea is copyrightable, but not the idea itself. As far as titles are concerned, there are at least two books called *Death in the Afternoon*; one's Hemingway's, one's mine. There are numerous books called *The Power and the Glory*. There are numerous books called *The Powers That Be*. There are numerous books called . . . Need I go on? Also uncopyrightable are works other people already have copyrighted, unless you succeed in convincing them or paying them to give you their copyright, which brings us to what both academic and commercial publishers often want you to do: give them what's yours.

"Academic authors rarely protest copyrighting in the press' name," says one professor with much publishing experience. "Nothing in the copyright law indicates that publishers have the automatic right to copyright books they publish. Yet many academics are so anxious to have a publication on their academic record within the year that they go ahead and permit heinous infringements of their rights. As long as publishers hold the copyright, they hold the right to discontinue the book and take it out of print. Why should they have that?" Many academics would reply that if they don't give up their copyright, their book won't get published. Your copyright's worth fighting for, though, especially if you don't mind making concessions in other areas. Giving up your copyright may solve some of your immediate problems, but may bring you face to face with other, larger problems later on.

"I'm beginning to wonder whether I should have insisted on retaining my copyright," says John Elliott of a book he coauthored, *Proclamation: Aids for Interpreting the Lessons of the Church Year, Pentecost 3, Series A* (Philadelphia: Fortress Press, 1975). "It's my work, the product of my labor, and I ought to have control of it. Not having the copyright indicates to me I really can't dispose of that work."

Elliott also wants to regain his copyright in his first book, *The Elect and the Holy,* but two publishers were involved, none of the people he originally negotiated with are still on the scene, and nobody seems able to give him a definitive answer. "I've given up," he says, even though the largest publisher of academic theological books in the country wanted to reprint the book and would have done so if Elliott could have regained the copyright. "As long as you've got a good relationship with your editor or publisher, everything's okay, but when you're working with an editor or publisher you don't know, turning everything over to the publisher seems questionable," Elliott says.

Of course, you're free to sell any of your property, but your first step is to be aware that you own it. Once you realize that, you can start thinking about what you should get in return for it. You might try finding out what rights in your work the publisher most cares about. Then give the publisher those specific rights for the specific period of time the publisher is interested in retaining them, rather than giving the publisher all your rights to your work.

Ideally, you will want to grant your publisher only the exclusive right to publish and sell your work in the United States, in return for specified fees and percentages, for a restricted period of time.

You give up a great deal by granting such rights to the publisher and should be paid for doing so. Nevertheless, by granting only such rights you have retained your rights to sell your manuscript as a magazine article, movie or videotape, computer disk, radio or television script, in other countries, or at other times. You give up such rights, and all others, when you sell your copyright.

Publishers want your copyright so they can gain whatever there is to be gained from publishing your work. If you give the publisher your copyright, you will only be able to regain those rights by buying them back, or pleading tearfully with the publisher to give them to you, until 40 long years go by. (Forty years after you granted the copyright to another, or 35 years after the date of publication of the work involved, whichever comes first. After that period, you can terminate the transfer of rights.)

At least when you sell your copyright, you know what you're losing: your copyright. You may not know what you're losing when you write your work as a "work for hire."

If you're a writer on a company payroll, a regular 9–5 employee, all your work done on the company's time becomes the company's property under the work-for-hire provision of the copyright law. Most folks would agree this makes sense. However, many publishers ask academic and other writers to sign work-for-hire agreements, treating their work as if they were full-time employees of the publisher. This means giving up their copyright and putting all future monetary benefits from their work into the company's hands, even when they're not full-time or part-time employees of the publisher.

Once you sign a work-for-hire agreement, your publisher can print or reprint part or all of your work an unlimited number of times in the same form, or in different forms or in different media, for as long as there's a market for it anywhere, without paying you a single additional penny. Just to add insult to injury, under a work-for-hire agreement the publisher has no obligation to even mention the author's name when publishing the work, since the publisher becomes the author by virtue of the agreement.

By signing a book contract containing a work-for-hire agreement, you give up every right you have in your work, as in this provision from an actual work-for-hire contract:

> The author acknowledges that the work is being specifically commissioned by the Editor and is to be prepared by the Contributor as a "work made for hire." The Contributor understands that the Publisher shall own all of the exclusive rights to the work under the United States copyright law and all international copyright conventions, including the right to copyright it and any renewals thereof in the name of the Publisher, the Editor, or their assignees.

Sign a contract bearing a clause containing this or any other work-for-hire provision and your manuscript joins Judge Crater in never-never land as far as any monetary benefits to you are concerned, except for the initial "fee for service" the publisher gives you.

Of course, your publisher may tell you outright, or strongly hint, that unless you sign a work-for-hire agreement, your book won't be published. Here's where you'll have to weigh the estimated value of your work against the estimated value to your academic career of getting it published.

You may well decide to assign many of your rights to your publisher. But in the long run, even if you want to sign some or all of your rights away, it's better to sign away each right specifically or transfer the copyright to the publisher than to sign a work-for-hire agreement. If you sign away some or all of your rights, at worst, 35–40 years later you're entitled to a reversion. This limit is written into the copyright law as a protection for authors. Now 35 years is a long time but at least it comes to an end; there's no end to this period if you sell your work as a work-for-hire. The publisher becomes the author; there's nothing for you to get back.

If you can avoid signing a work-for-hire agreement, you'll be able to get everything back in 35 years. What's 35 years when you're trying to write a work that will live forever?

Chapter 10

INDEXES AND OTHER DANGERS

> *So essential did I consider an index to be to every book, that I proposed to bring a bill into Parliament to deprive an author who publishes a book without an index of the privilege of copyright, and, moreover, to subject him, for his offense, to a pecuniary penalty.*
> —*Baron Campbell, 1745*

Robert Elias wanted to do the index for his book, *The Politics of Victimization,* although he was "pretty tired" from all his work on the book itself. But his publisher convinced Elias that the book would come out much better with the publisher's professional indexer working on it. Elias agreed, but still wanted to provide some guidance.

"I sent them a copy of the manuscript on which I had highlighted all the key words I thought would be appropriate in the index," Elias explains. "The indexer competely ignored it. They came up with a horrible index and charged me $600 for it (to be taken out of royalties.) I got that down a couple of hundred dollars but still didn't want the index that had been put together. I was on vacation at the time and spent four days with a friend putting a new index together. Then they said they couldn't use it because it was too long, but I fought them on that and won."

As this incident indicates, the additional materials that make up a book, such as indexes, illustrations, music scores, and maps, can create at least as much trouble between author and publisher as the book itself.

By the time proofreading and indexing time roll around, the publisher's book production machine is in high gear and the publisher wants action fast. The author's days of leisurely manuscript compilation out by the pool are over. Authors may either have to do an index fast or have someone else do it, with the cost taken out of the author's royalties.

But there is a better way. If the publisher wants you to do the index, ask for a larger advance or a larger royalty payment. If the publisher wants to hire someone else to do it, try to convince the publisher to pick up the tab or most of it and charge your share to your royalty account, rather than requiring you to pay cash for the index. By all means limit your index-related liability to $500.

Remember when negotiating this point, however, that professional indexers charge the publisher $1.85-$2.50 per book page to compile a name and subject index. It may be worth this cost (whoever pays it) to hire a professional indexer, since a professional indexer understands how people crucial to your book's success, such as librarians and reviewers, will evaluate your book's index. If you go the professional indexer route, though, be sure to ask to see the completed index, since you know the book better than anyone else and will be able to spot any mistakes the indexer may have made. Check the index rapidly; the publisher will need it returned shortly.

You also should attempt to limit your liability in terms of the number of photographs or illustrations you provide. If any of these are copyrighted, permissions must be obtained, and often paid for. In the case of a heavily illustrated book, merely requesting the permissions can mean almost as much work as writing the text. It can also cost you, one way or another, more than your advance.

"We were so naive and stupid," says Beverly Guy-Sheftall. "Three of us were editors of one book. The advance was approximately $3,000 to be divided among us. But what we had to pay for permissions came out of the advance. So we never got any money for doing the book."

To avoid such an outcome, suggest the following clause or a similar one for your contract:

The author agrees to furnish the following additional materials: _____ . (Insert an approximate number of photos, pictures, or whatever, to avoid future disputes with the publisher.)

Then try to get one of the following clauses included, in descending order of preference.

Best for you:
The publisher agrees to obtain permissions to use material copyrighted by others and to pay for such permissions. Such payments shall not be considered advances against royalties.

Second best for you:
The author will obtain permissions to use material copyrighted by others. The publisher will pay the fees for such permissions and shall not hold these as advances against royalties.

Third best for you:
The author will obtain permissions to use material copyrighted by others. The author will pay half the fees for such permissions, up to $ _____ . The publisher shall pay the remainder and shall not hold this cost as an advance against royalties.

Don't be surprised if your publisher agrees to include one of the clauses above, although the publisher may want to put an upper limit on its liability.

Some of these permissions arrangements may become complicated, but they also may become beneficial for the author.

For earlier editions of one of his books, David McCurdy and his publisher agreed that if permissions cost $10,000 or less, the publisher and McCurdy would each pay half the cost. On one later edition of the same book, with the ceiling still $10,000, the publisher agreed to pay the first $5,000 and McCurdy agreed to pay anything in addition to that. But since the permissions cost less than $10,000, McCurdy's publisher's share was larger than McCurdy's (which was in any case subtracted from his royalties rather than paid directly). In fact, some publishers pay extra for original illustrations or photographs by the author. But don't ask for such an additional payment at the last moment. Have it in your contract from the beginning.

Chapter 11

SUBSIDIARY RIGHTS: THE BIGGEST PART IS UNDERWATER

Film option: The pittance they pay you now for the
right to rip you off later.

—*Anonymous*

Commercial presses are more and more concerned with publishing only those books for which subsidiary rights—periodical, bookclub, paperback, foreign language, TV, and motion picture rights—can be sold for big bucks. University presses tend to publish books without blockbuster subsidiary potential, but remember that no one can predict the future of any book. Ohio State University Press published *". . . And Ladies of the Club"* by Helen Hooven Santmyer in 1982, then sold the paperback and trade rights to G. P. Putnam's Sons for $250,000. *". . . And Ladies of the Club"* went on to be a main selection of the Book-of-the-Month Club. *The Hunt for Red October*, by Tom Clancy, published by the Naval Institute Press in 1984, became a major motion picture starring Sean Connery. The book *Storyville, New Orleans, Being an Authentic, Illustrated Account of the Notorious Red-Light District*, by Al Rose, published by the University of Alabama Press in 1974, became the basis for the motion picture *Pretty Baby* with Brooke Shields.

So don't let anyone tell you not to concern yourself with the provisions in your book contract dealing with the sale of subsidiary rights of your book. Even if it doesn't become a best seller, your academic book, whether published by a commercial or an academic press, may earn you—or your publisher—a fairly large amount of money through sale of paperback and other rights. It's not at all unusual, for example, for a commercial press to buy the paperback rights to a university press book, or for a commercial or academic press to buy the rights to publish part of a university press book in an anthology.

Usually your publisher will want the right to sell your periodical rights (the right to publish part or all of your book in a periodical), bookclub rights, and paperback rights. Your publisher will also sometimes want the right to sell your foreign language rights and British Commonwealth rights. If you or your agent think you will be able to do a better job of selling any of these rights than the publisher, by all means suggest you keep those rights. If you have no agent, don't want to do any selling, and don't think the subsidiary rights will be worth much, you might want to leave all of them with the publisher. But try to get the highest possible percentage of what the publisher will be paid for the rights.

Protect yourself with a clause such as:

> The author grants to the publisher the exclusive right to license or sell the following subsidiary rights: _____ , with the author's written consent, which shall not be unreasonably withheld.

If you're able to insert this clause in your contract, it will give you initial control over which rights are sold and eventual control over the price at which those rights are sold, since you can always withhold your consent until the price is right.

Most contracts specify the percentage of each subsidiary right sold that will go to you and the percentage that will go to your publisher. Since you wrote the book, you should be the primary beneficiary of any subsidiary sales. Nevertheless, most publishers ask for at least 50 percent of the amount they receive for the sale of each and every subsidiary right. You should push in the other direction. Aim at getting 90 percent for yourself from the sale of first serial (periodical) rights, 75 percent for United Kingdom and foreign language rights, and 50–66 percent of the sale price of all other rights.

Don't assume foreign rights to your book aren't worth anything, especially if you're writing about foreign countries.

B. J. Chandler's first book, *The Feitosas and the Sertao dos Inhamuns*, published by the University of Florida Press in 1972, was later published by a university press in Brazil. At Chandler's urging, Florida agreed to give the book to the Brazilian university press at no cost. But the book did well in Brazil—two printings, 8,000 copies—causing Florida to regret its Chandler-inspired generosity, Chandler says.

Sometimes, however, it's difficult for either author or publisher to obtain the funds they may be owed by foreign publishers. Chandler's book *Bandit King*, originally published by Texas A&M Press, was republished by a commercial publisher in Rio de Janiero in 1981. The contract between that publisher and A&M had royalty provisions, "but it was extremely difficult to get the money out of the Brazilian publisher," Chandler says. "After a long period, they paid, I think, $1,250 that A&M had asked as an initial payment. There was also a provision for royalties to be paid on subsequent printings. But last I knew, the book, which was about Brazil's major bandit figure, had gone through four or five printings, had sold more than 20,000 copies, and was on the Brazilian best seller list—and I never got any royalty payments."

Try also to avoid giving your publisher the motion picture, TV, merchandising, and commercial tie-in rights, or seek to retain 90 percent of the proceeds of the sale of those rights for yourself. Remember that while the publisher may work hard to sell some of those rights, the publisher may also dispose of some of them merely by accepting a phoned-in offer.

If no subsidiary rights are sold, it doesn't matter how fast you get the money from such sales: getting $0 tomorrow is no different from getting $0 next year, except for tax purposes. But if such rights *are* sold, you'll want to get your share of the money as quickly as possible. You might try to insert a provision in your contract requiring the publisher to send you your share of the subsidiary rights money without applying that money to the as yet unearned portion of your advance. Although it's unlikely the publisher will agree to this, you might try backing off a half-step by seeking to apply this provision only to some of the rights rather than to all of them.

If that doesn't work, you should try to insert a provision requiring the subsidiary rights money to come to you within a specified period, once your advance has been paid, rather than waiting for such money to be included in your yearly royalty checks. Such a provision might read:

> Once the advance has been repaid, the author's share (when it amounts to over $500) of all monies received for subsidiary rights shall be paid to him or her within 14 days of their receipt by the publisher.

Random House has agreed to such arrangements, so why not your publisher?

Chapter 12

DEALING WITH EDITORS AND OTHER STRANGERS

> *When the editor who bought the book leaves the company before the book is published, the winds blow very cold. In the trade, such a book is called an "orphan," and the word barely suggests the Dickensian—nay, the Hogarthian—horrors that await such a creature. Who shall defend these pitiful pages? Who shall raise this tattered banner from the Out basket? No one.*
> —*From* A Likely Story *by Donald Westlake*
> *(New York: Mysterious Press, 1984)*

Your editor can be your best friend. Your editor can tell you what's wrong with your manuscript or can point out mistakes and misjudgments you've made that no one else will point out to you, because they live with you or brought you up or fear hurting you.

Your editor can also tell you what's good about your manuscript, and encourage you to bring out more of whatever that is. Allow the editor to do so. If you disagree with the changes an editor makes in your manuscript, say so. But don't get emotional. Defend your objections rationally. Try to make it clear to the editor that you believe that the two of you should work together to make the book as good as it possibly can be.

And don't take editing personally; your book is not you. It's only one of many things you have done or will do with your life. Anyway, would you rather (a) be edited well or (b) see colleagues shake their heads and giggle derisively while reading your book because they can't understand what you've written.

After your proposal or partial manuscript has been accepted by a publishing house, find out who your editor is. Contact and establish a rapport with this editor. Indicate that you're willing to make any changes in the manuscript the editor thinks are necessary (as long as they aren't contrary to your principles or to your deepest sense of what your manuscript should be). The earlier you get advice or suggestions from your editor, the less rewriting you'll have to do later. Make sure both of you agree on the aim of the book. If you do, the disagreements on principle that divide you should be very few.

Ask if, as you finish each significant part of your manuscript, you may send it to your editor to make certain you both agree on where the book's going. If you plan to make changes in the way you approach your subject or in the structure of your manuscript, let the editor know and get a reaction to your proposed changes.

One thing your editor is likely to try to protect you and the publishing house against is libel: the damage to a person's reputation from something you wrote about that person in your book that brings the person into hatred, contempt, or ridicule in the eyes of a substantial and respectable group. Many book contracts require the author to guarantee that a manuscript "contains no matter whatsoever that is obscene, libelous, in violation of any right of privacy, or otherwise in contravention of law or the right of any third party."

Responsible editors will help you rid your manuscript of any libelous statements inadvertently included in it. Nevertheless, inadvertent libel occurs, and when it occurs, it's often expensive, especially if the entire expense falls on you, the author. Many book contracts require the author to pay any legal fees or damages resulting from a charge of libel against the author's book. No need to scream in horror; there is at least one way around this vast and soggy pit: libel insurance, which many publishers have purchased. The least you can do for yourself is arrange to be covered by that insurance. Such an arrangement is acceptable to many publishers.

Try to insert the following language in your contract:

The publisher agrees to obtain author insurance coverage

against copyright, libel, or any other lawsuit that may be brought against the author and/or publisher. In the event that judgment is made against the author, all court and legal expenses and damages in excess of _____ (the amount of the deductible) shall be paid by such insurance.

Even if your publishing house grants you such coverage, be wary, as with any other insurance plan, of the size of the deductible, the ceiling on payments from the plan, and any loopholes the plan may contain. Some deductibles are so high—$100,000 or more—that putting the above clause in your contract wouldn't be worth the effort unless the publisher will agree to pay the deductible. Naturally, if the publisher won't pay the deductible in a case involving your book, the lower the deductible the better. Your best bet would be to convince the publisher to agree to pay the entire deductible, but you're more likely to convince the publisher to agree to an arrangement similar to the many arrangements between publishers and authors in the area of permission fees. That is, the publisher will agree to pay 50 percent of all libel and court costs up to X number of dollars, and 100 percent of everything thereafter. Random House limits its authors' liability to 10 percent of their advance, obviously a desirable goal for every author.

Ask the publisher to send you a copy of the publisher's libel insurance plan, if carried, and make sure the small print in the plan doesn't waive coverage for certain sorts of libel or plagiarism suits. Too many exceptions and the plan is a dodo bird. And keep your eye on the ceiling. This is the publisher's insurance, not yours, so a ceiling of $1 million a year may be worth a lot less than you think if your publisher is forced to defend more than one libel suit during the same year. And remember, if you never get to this stage because your publisher rejects your final manuscript as too risky legally, you may be entitled to your manuscript and all rights to it back without being obliged to return any of your advance.

Discussing how your book will be edited and the possibility of libel being edited out assumes that the publishing house that has accepted your manuscript wants to edit your book well, or edit it at all. Some do. Some don't. Some assign careless editors to the task. As a recent article in *American Scholar* put it, referring to legendary editor Maxwell Perkins, "Mistah Perkins—He dead!"

Bad or nonexistent editing is such a widespread phenomenon these days that you should try to get a provision in your contract stating that your publisher has an obligation to edit your manuscript, provide you with written editorial guidance, and proofread your book. Although this is a writer's right and has been upheld by the courts, in *Goldwater v. Harcourt Brace Jovanovich* and *Dell v. Weldon*, your editor may refuse to look at your manuscript while it is in progress. Your publisher may then tell you the final manuscript is unacceptable and the house won't publish it. It will be much more difficult for a publishing house to make this claim if its editor has been editing and commenting on your work all along.

It's also possible that while the publishing house may accept your final manuscript, the house will try to save money by not editing it, or by charging you for the editing. After all, in Paul Lipke's words, "Editing takes a lot of work. To be sensitive to what the author's trying to say, to clarify points, to restructure, takes care and love and time. That's why good editors often burn out," and, in part, why some publishing houses do very little editing.

"I've worked for publications that couldn't leave a single sentence alone," Lipke says, but as for others, "You make a typo [in the manuscript], you see the typo in print."

You don't want this, or any variant thereof, to happen to you. Ask that the following language be included in your contract:

> The publisher shall provide the author with written editorial guidance, line editing, and proofreading in preparing the book for publication.

You may not have much trouble getting this in your contract. What publishing house wants to admit it doesn't edit or proofread its manuscripts?

But corporate shenanigans can play havoc with a manuscript, especially if they cause a change in editors. As many writers have learned to their cost, editors sometimes quit or are fired while the book they are editing is in preparation. The book then becomes an "orphan" and is handed over to some editor who has a completely different conception of what it should be about or simply doesn't give a damn about it. It's hard to protect yourself against such a disaster, but losing your editor is a much greater catastrophe than most authors realize. So why not try for some protection? Urge that the following clauses be included in your contract:

a. If for any reason the editor becomes disassociated from the project during the creation, production, or early promotion of the book, the publisher and the author shall together select a new editor for the book.

b. In the event that after a good-faith effort is made by both parties, the author and the publisher cannot agree on a choice of editor, the writer shall have the right to terminate this contract and all rights shall return to the writer. Monies previously paid to the writer shall be repaid to the publisher from and to the extent of the first proceeds from the resale of the book.

It will be difficult to convince a publisher to include these clauses in your contract. And even if you do succeed in having them inserted, you ought to avoid invoking Paragraph b unless your ship is definitely on the way to the bottom and you're unable to break the chain attaching you to your oar.

Once you invoke this paragraph, you'll have to sell your book again. And since you'll have to repay whatever you received of your first advance from your second advance, you won't be paid twice for your effort. If the editor newly assigned to you is enthusiastic about you and your book, don't exercise your option. However, with this paragraph in your contract, if you find yourself and your book in a true orphan situation, you'll have a handy hacksaw to use.

In any case, the paragraph does establish that it's the publisher's job to make sure you have a good editor. It also saves you from having to repay any monies to the publisher you leave behind until you've resold your manuscript to your bright new publisher.

Even if you stay with the same publisher, when you're assigned a new editor, any agreements you made with your old editor will go out the door with that editor unless they're memorialized in your contract.

"They told me they'd publish my book [*The Politics of Victimization*] as both a trade and an academic book," Robert Elias says. "Then they marketed it as an academic book only. They didn't put it on their trade list and never told me why not. When I asked, they just said, 'We decided against it.' Part of it was the change in editors. 'I don't know what she told you,' the new editor said, 'but we didn't think it would be good for the trade list.' " That's why you want to have all agreements in your contract.

COVERS

Few if any authors are granted the right to approve (or disapprove) the covers of their books. Publishers usually point out that the author has had much less experience with publishing book covers than the publisher has.

The publisher, according to this argument, has been able to gauge marketplace reaction to many different covers, while the author has not had such experience.

Nevertheless, publishing houses would do well to consult authors about proposed cover designs. Some publishing houses do. Some don't.

"My book has the ugliest cover you could imagine, even though I sent repeated letters to the publisher pleading, 'Just let me see the cover you're going to use,'" Elias says. "Instead the book just showed up one day with this horrible cover. It was orangy yellow with my name and the name of the book written in very stark letters as if I had done it in the basement myself. No design. When I asked, they said, 'It was a stark topic so we thought we'd use a stark cover.' They said they'd change it in the second printing, but when it came out, they hadn't changed it. Nothing in the contract gave me control."

It wasn't only the cover that gave Elias pause.

"They also had agreed to typeset the tables," he says, "but then decided to use a much less professional form for those tables, so the nice type in the book doesn't match the type in the tables. A lot of these things were less a matter of doing something malicious and more a matter of poor communications, change of personnel, disarray in editorial offices, and editors' assistants coming and going."

If Elias had had the right of veto or at least consultation over such matters written into his contract, he probably would not have had as much cause for complaint.

If the art work, design, and jacket of your book are as important to you as they are to most authors, don't make Elias' mistake. And if you can gather prepublication endorsements of your manuscript from leaders in your field, by all means send them to your editor and suggest one or more of them be included in the cover design. Also convey, politely but enthusiastically, any ideas you may have for a design or blurbs for your cover. Do so early, so your ideas can be taken into account.

You would be best off with a guaranteed veto or right of approval, but you may well have to settle for consultation. Try to insert

The author shall have the right of approval on such production matters as cover design, layout, art work, advertising, and promotional copy.

into your contract. If the publisher won't agree, try for

> The publisher agrees to consult comprehensively with the author on such production matters as cover design, layout, advertising, and promotional copy.

Chapter 13

WILL IT BE IN BOOKSTORES? WILL ANYONE KNOW IT'S THERE?

> *[Confederate General Longstreet meets Confeder-*
> *ate General Pettigrew on the last day of the battle*
> *of Gettysburg]: Longstreet: "They tell me you've*
> *written a book." Pettigrew: "Yes, sir..." Long-*
> *street: "What was it about?" Pettigrew: "Oh, it*
> *was only a minor work, sir." Longstreet: "I'll have*
> *to read it." Pettigrew: "You will have a copy, sir,*
> *with my compliments." To Longstreet's surprise,*
> *Pettigrew rose, summoned an aide, and dispatched*
> *the man for the book.*
> —From The Killer Angels, *by Michael Shaara*
> *(New York: Ballantine Books, 1974)*

University presses have become more aggressive publiciz-ers in recent years, according to Paul Parsons in *Getting Published.* They advertise in major publications and specialty journals and in brochures distributed at academic conventions. They send out news releases. Their sales representatives visit bookstores and offer discounts on bulk purchases. They send direct-mail brochures; they buy mailing lists. Some even market their books jointly.

In spite of such efforts, author complaints about lack of publicity for their books remain numerous.

"There was no promotion of my book," Beverly Guy-Sheftall says of her book *Sturdy Black Bridges: Visions of Black Women in Literature,* "but I understand that's fairly common."

"My publisher didn't promote my book," notes Karen Brodkin Sacks about one of her books. "I wanted it displayed at anthropology meetings and meetings of other disciplines, and ads taken out in women's studies journals and other periodicals. But the publisher didn't do it."

Her publisher's response to the complaints: every author feels that way.

"They said I wasn't getting bad treatment," Sacks says. "But sales were pretty bad. So bad, in fact, that they couldn't justify putting the book out in paperback."

"For my second book [*Langston Hughes: Before and Beyond Harlem* (Westport: Lawrence Hill & Co., 1983)], "I depended for publicity on reviews and book parties," Faith Berry says. "The book received unnanimously good reviews in over 40 publications throughout the country, but my publisher didn't want to pay to send me to those places to promote the book, so I lost many sales I could have had."

This situation is partly the result of the large number of books published by both commercial and university presses and their scattergun approach to book publishing: many books are published, but those that get some attention on their own are given most of the publicity muscle while the rest are ignored and die.

"Knopf did a pretty good publicity job for my book," says Sara Evans about her *Personal Politics: The Roots of Women's Liberation in the Civil Rights Movement and the New Left.* "It got nice review attention. But the same month my book came out Lauren Bacall's autobiography came out, and that got the big push."

Another problem: unrealistically high author expectations often make even sufficient publicity seem like too little.

There are several solutions to these problems. One is insisting on provisions for a guaranteed promotional allowance and advertising expenditures in your book contract. What will also help is making it clear that you'll be eager and available to help publicize your own book at the appropriate academic conventions, or on radio and television talk shows in and out of town.

If you're planning to attend a professional or academic convention at which your book might be sold, urge your publisher to make the book available at the convention and

100

volunteer to help promote it there, meet people interested in it, sign copies, or take whatever action is appropriate to help sell the book. After all, for each book sold, the publisher will receive a much larger percentage of the cover price than you will, so a publisher is quite likely to be grateful for your (unpaid) efforts on his or her behalf.

If you're going to the convention anyway, your efforts on behalf of your book there, although unpaid, will cost you nothing and may gain you recognition as well as sales. You might even want to gamble some of your own money on attending a convention you might not otherwise have attended in order to attract attention to your book. If you get an offer of a better job out of your efforts, as well as draw more attention to your book, you'll feel highly repaid.

Unfortunately, many book promo horror stories revolve around authors pleading with their publishers to send a couple of hundred copies to the appropriate convention, flying there at their own expense to promote the book, and then waiting chin in hand for the books, which arrive the day after the convention ends.

Howard Wachtel was due to lecture on international economics at a seminar on public policy for a senior government officials' group in Denver. The group wanted to buy twenty copies of his recently published book, *The Money Mandarins*, but could get only three. Wachtel called his publisher and suggested the books be sent via United Parcel Service. The publisher already had the book order in hand, but, says Wachtel, "they were never able to get the books out there."

REVIEW COPIES AND REVIEWS

You should cooperate with your publisher's efforts to determine which journals and individuals should be sent review copies. Authors usually know more about this than the publisher's marketing people, who are often eager for assistance in this area. Try to get a clause in your contract guaranteeing you close consultation on publicity and marketing strategy. You should also push for a clause requiring the publisher to make available a specific number of complimentary review and promotion copies of the book to be sent out at your request and direction. Point out that better publicity is in everyone's interest.

Sara Evans says she and the University of Chicago press agreed in her book contract on the various kinds of direct mail Chicago would send out to help her book reach its audience. Chicago agreed to send mail to people on parts of the lists of various organizations and to people working in personnel and other specific areas. (The book was *Wage Justice: Comparable Worth and the Paradox of Technocratic Reform* [Chicago: University of Chicago Press, 1989], which Evans coauthored with Barbara J. Nelson.)

You should also let your publisher know if any events occur in your personal or professional life that could be used as publicity for the book: your election to a major academic post, for instance, or the verification of your cold-fusion experiment.

In an ideal world, your publisher will pay for promotion of your book. In the decidedly non-ideal world of academic and commercial publishing, the publisher may do so on your first book but is much more likely to do so on your second and subsequent books (if your first book does well). Try to get a dollar figure into your contract specifying the minimum amount that the publisher will spend on promotion and advertising of your book. If you're unable to insert such a clause in your contract and your publisher won't spend what you consider a sufficient amount, you might consider taking your own fate in your own hands, as Wachtel did with *The Money Mandarins.*

"My book was given a full-page review in *Business Week,* which reviews one book a week," says Wachtel. "I was on 20 or 30 radio and television shows, including the 'Larry King Show.' A United Press International story focused entirely on me and the book and criticisms it made of the Reagan administration. A column about the book by Robert Walters appeared in 200 small papers throughout country. I was on CNN's 'International

Hour' with Bernard Shaw, 'All Things Considered,' 'Morning Edition,' and local and regional call-in talk shows. I thought I had hit the big time. But none of this came through the publisher's publicity people. I arranged it all myself."

You, too, can promote your book on your own. To do so with any success, you will want to obtain as many free copies from the publisher as possible. If it's compatible with your dignity, you might even try selling the books yourself. Author Alexander Cockburn crisscrossed America on a low-budget book tour in 1989, publicizing his book *The Fate of the Forest: Developers, Destroyers and Defenders of the Amazon* (New York: Verso, 1989), which he coauthored with UCLA ecologist Susanna Hecht. Verso had no publicity budget, so Cockburn paid his own way. He often avoided lodging expenses by staying with friends or with local activist groups who took up collections for his expenses. He also earned back some of his tour expenses through lecture fees.

Not everyone's book is promotable in this way, but if yours is, you might want to try it, especially if you can do your tour as part of a sabbatical or a vacation. If you've written a book specifically applicable to a number of localities, you might want to ask your publisher to send you around to those locales as part of your campaign. Gary Kyriazi, the author of *The Great American Amusement Parks: A Pictorial History* (Secaucus: Citadel Press, 1976), gathered acres of free publicity by visiting towns with amusement parks and rating each of those parks in comparison with others nationwide, while reporters from local newspapers took notes and cameras from the local TV stations whirred. After all, he was the expert: he had written the book on the subject.

Even Dan Greenburg, the well-known and successful author of such best-sellers as *How to Be a Jewish Mother* and *How to Make Yourself Miserable*, routinely phones bookstores to suggest they stock his new title. His publishers won't do it, so Greenburg does it himself.

103

Other authors buy up the entire first printing of their book and drive around the country placing copies in bookstores. Some authors call up talk shows, pretend to be from the XYZ Public Relations firm, and book themselves a spot on the show. Many hire their own publicity firms to perform the same task.

So push for language in your contract that will give you 25 free copies of each edition, as well as the right to purchase copies of the work at 50 percent of retail or at the lowest discounted price offered by the publisher, whichever is less.

And if you think your book is of widespread general interest and has real sales potential, hire your own publicist. Better yet, try to get a clause in your contract allowing you to use the publisher's money to hire a publicist acceptable to the publisher.

Unfortunately, when publishers or publishing units merge, publicity fails or falters. Jack Weatherford said his publisher, Rawson, Wade, an imprint of Scribners, was doing an outstanding publicity job on his book, *Tribes On the Hill: An Investigation into the Rituals and Realities of an Endangered American Species, the Congress of the United States* (New York: Rawson, Wade, 1981).

Then one week before the book was to come out, Weatherford said, Scribners "collapsed Rawson, Wade back into itself and fired everyone I was working with, including the publicity director. I had been booked for the Today Show. Then I was bumped from the show but I didn't have a publicity director any more to get me back on. I fell between the cracks. Scribners nominally assigned someone as a PR agent for the book, but the agent never booked a single appearance and wrote a press release calling me *James* Weatherford and calling the book *Tribes of the Hill.* It was a catastrophe."

Sometimes disputes between publisher and author over the nature of the publicity required for a particular book may derail even a well-intentioned promotional effort. Weatherford's second publisher gave his second book the title *Porn Row: An Inside Look at the Sex-for-Sale District of a Major American City*

(New York: Arbor House, 1986). Weatherford's proposed title was *Junk Food Sex*. (The book was later published in Japan as *The Fast Food Love* [Tokyo: Kousaido Shuppan, 1989]).

"I emphasized the whole district and everything that went on in it, including drugs, crime and fencing of stolen goods," Weatherford says. "The publisher emphasized pornography. I had a problem with doing that sort of publicity. As soon as I would get on the show, the show would either head to people's personal sexual problems, and there was nothing I could say about those, or would go to a political argument about whether pornography should be banned or not. I did a couple of shows, like Dr. Ruth, but then stopped. I didn't want to get involved in people's personal lives, and I was divided between the First Amendment, which I support strongly, and not wanting to make more money for pornographers."

Sometimes a decent promotional effort can be derailed by circumstances. Arthur Quinn's publisher heavily promoted his first book, *Before Abraham Was*, which Quinn coauthored with Isaac Kikawada. The religion editor of *Time* magazine even wrote a story on the book and Quinn was told that if the section had room in the next month or so the story would run. But a series of important religion stories occurred over the next month, so the piece on Quinn's book never appeared.

Chapter 14

REPRINTS AND REMAINDERINGS: THERE IS LIFE AFTER TERMINATION

No one has ever walked into a bookstore and asked for the latest Random House.

—Anonymous

Very few book contracts include any requirement that the publisher publish the book in any particular format (hardcover, trade paperback, mass market paperback), publish any particular number of copies, keep the book in print for any particular length of time, reprint it after its initial printing, or publish a second edition. A publisher may sell paperback rights to another company or just sit on the book after publishing the initial edition.

You should try to convey your views on such matters to your publisher. After all, in most senses the book that is published will be your book rather than the publisher's. No one ever walked into a bookstore and asked for the latest Random House. So you ought to have some say about the format in which your book will appear. You might even know something about your particular part of the academic market that the publisher doesn't know.

Very few authors are able to convince publishers to make written commitments in these areas. But try discussing these issues with your publisher up front. As a result of such a conversation, at least you might discover what your publisher has in mind, which can't hurt. At best, assuming you have a choice among publishers, one prospective publisher's paperback and second edition plans may convince you to sign with that publisher rather than with the one whose plans in those areas don't appeal to you.

You should ask your publisher what criteria must be satisfied to justify a second edition. If the answer is vague (criteria may change over time and from book to book), you should check the publisher's catalogue and see which books have gone into subsequent editions. You could then find out from the authors the sales and publishing history of each of those books. This sort of information is not as firm as contractual language, of course, but it's better than nothing and may give you a fairly accurate picture of what your publisher's plans might be for your book.

Most academic authors assume their books will be published in hardcover first, and in paperback later, if at all. After all, hardcover books are taken more seriously and reviewed more often. And from a purely mercenary point of view, it makes sense to both author and publisher to publish, say, a required textbook in hardcover, because the price is higher, and the royalty percentage and the price on which that percentage is calculated are higher.

Hardcover publication may even make sense to students, if they can sell their used hardcover for a better price than the used paperback version would sell for, or if they want to keep the book for later use. And from the author's point of view, while hardcovers are often reprinted as paperbacks, few books originally printed as paperbacks are reprinted as hardcovers.

However, there are advantages to having your book published initially as a paperback. Although its cover price, as well as your royalty percentage, will be lower, your book's sales may be higher and your book may be adopted more often as a required or supplementary text because of that lower price. You and your publisher might also consider simultaneous hardcover and paperback publication (hardcovers for instructors and libraries, paperbacks for students). You should try to find out when, if ever, the publisher plans to publish a paperback edition or whether the publisher plans to sell the paperback rights rather than publish it in paperback.

If you're interested in even medium-term immortality, you might also ask if your book will be printed on acid-free paper rather than on acidic paper that will self-destruct fifty years after publication.

The paperback versus hardcover question becomes more relevant for academics as universities publish more books with widespread rather than strictly scholarly appeal, books that more often appear in paperback. Those same university presses are increasingly reprinting their own hardcovers in paperback or printing hardcover and paperback editions simultaneously, rather than selling the paperback rights to other publishers, the traditional practice.

Authors occasionally complain that publishers are too quick to publish a book in paperback while it is selling well in hardcover. More often, though, the author complains that the publisher never bothered with a paperback edition, even though the book sold well enough in hardcover to justify one.

"My publisher promised me orally they'd do a paperback edition of *The Money Mandarins*, and then never did one," says Howard Wachtel. "They sold all the hardbound copies and let the book go out of print. They didn't even sell the paperback rights to anyone else, in spite of all the publicity the book got. So after the book went out of print and the contract expired, I got the rights back."

It's common for a publisher to let the stock of hardcover copies of a book run out, not print a paperback edition, and not sell the paperback rights; to refuse to print a second or third edition of a book; or to refuse to order a second printing of the first edition. Sometimes the author has reserved, through language inserted in the contract, the paperback or second edition rights, or the right to sell the book elsewhere after it goes out of print. In many cases, even if such rights are not reserved for the author in the original contract, the author can request and will often receive the return of such rights, along with the plates or film of the book.

There are many reasons a second press may be interested in reprinting a book an original publisher no longer wants. The first press may no longer be publishing in that field while the second press is trying to get established in the same field, or the second publisher may have been established to handle books with limited press runs distributed only to a limited audience. Don't allow yourself to be bamboozled into accepting a substandard contract for the reprinted book just because you're grateful to get it back into print. If reprinting your book wasn't to the publisher's advantage in some way or another, the publisher wouldn't do it. And the author often gives the reprint house a precious gift: an already edited and proofread manuscript that has proven itself in the marketplace. Since the author often gives the second publisher the plates or the film for the book, the new publisher may not even need to reset the type for the book.

Two of Arthur Quinn's books were reprinted by second publishers after their original publishers let them go out of print. Abingdon originally printed his book *Before Abraham Was*, which was widely reviewed and well received, but, after sales dropped to about 1,000 copies a year, decided against a third printing. Ignatius Press in San Francisco acquired the book and republished it in 1989.

"I just showed the Ignatius Press people the sales figures," says Quinn. The plates were still available "for a song" from the original publisher, which made the second publisher's reprinting job a relatively easy one.

Some books are allowed to go out of print without an author's permission or even knowledge, especially if the author has nothing in the contract requiring he or she be notified when the book is about to be remaindered—sold by the publisher at a huge discount to a book discounter—or otherwise removed from list-price circulation. Authors in these cases only realize their book has been remaindered when they encounter huge piles of their $29.50 epics selling for $2.25 each on the sale table in the campus bookstore. Even then, without a contractual provision pertaining to remaindering, there's nothing much an author can do.

"The publisher didn't even inform us that our book was going out of print," says Beverly Guy-Sheftall. "They shredded the book and didn't even let us get at the extra copies."

"I've had three publishers who dropped books—let them go out of print—but never let me know," David McCurdy says. "In one case it took the publisher a year to acknowledge the book was out of print. I couldn't get copies myself and was getting calls from people who couldn't obtain it. I suspect they let it go out of stock but didn't make a policy decision to knock it out of print for a while. For a year and a half or so, I gave people the right to xerox the book for nothing and hoped to get the book reprinted. People who wanted it reprinted called the publishers and lobbied for the reprinting."

Sometimes, of course, if a book has gone into a second edition, it makes sense to remainder copies of the first edition. In any case, sooner or later almost every book gets remaindered. Such deep discounting is bad for the author because in most contracts, once the publisher begins selling the book at a 51 percent or greater discount, the author's royalties drop precipitously.

You want to (a) avoid premature remaindering, (b) retain the right to buy the remaindered books at the same price as the discounter (if you want to try selling them yourself) and (c) retain the right to buy the plates or film cheaply, in case another publisher wants to reprint your book.

Suggest the following clauses for your book contract:

There shall be no sale of overstock (copies sold in the U.S. at more than 70 percent discount) during the first 18 months after publication. The publisher shall notify the author at least 30 days before the book is remaindered, and give the author the opportunity to buy the overstock at a price no greater than the lowest price available to discount book sellers.

The publisher shall pay the author at least 10 percent of the price received for sale of such overstock unless the sale is made at or below manufacturing cost.

111

Should the publisher wish to destroy overstock, it shall give timely notice to the author, who may obtain any portion of the overstock by paying shipping costs.

Publishers occasionally donate books they no longer want to sell (overstock) to a charity, thereby gaining a large tax write off for themselves. Although there's nothing wrong with charity, you wrote the book and should attempt to put yourself in a position to receive some financial benefit from such a donation. Give yourself some protection by asking for the following clause in your contract:

The publisher may not give away overstock without the written permission of the author.

If this clause is in your contract and the publisher asks you for such permission, decide on something reasonable you want, then ask the publisher to give it to you in return for your written permission. All's fair in love and publishing.

Questions of overstock and premature remaindering aside, in the fullness of time, or in a much shorter time dictated by lack of sales, your book may be terminated. It's vitally necessary to insert a few paragraphs pertaining to this situation in your contract.

If you don't insert these paragraphs, your book, now dormant and well on its way to being outdated and forgotten, may be tied up in litigation for years before you can bring it to life once again.

The solution? Try to insert the following language in your contract:

If, at any time before or after the publication of the work, any of the following events occur:

a. The publisher notifies the author that the publisher intends to discontinue publication of the work; or

112

b. The publisher allows all U.S. editions of the work to go out of print—has no copies of the work available and offered for sale through normal retail channels, or does not list the work in the catalogue of the publisher and allows this condition to continue for more than 60 days; or

c. The publisher sells fewer than _____ copies of the work in a single year, this agreement shall terminate immediately, and all the publisher's rights to the work, subject to licenses previously granted, shall immediately revert to the author. The author shall have the right to buy the book's plates at a price no greater than 25 percent of their cost of manufacture and remaining copies bound or unbound at a price no greater than the lowest discounted price.

There are worse things than your book being terminated. Your hometown could be nuked. Or your publisher could go bankrupt.

Although your publisher cannot automatically terminate your contract if this happens, your publisher may opt to sell off your contract to satisfy creditors and you may lose all the money or royalties owed you as a result.

Perhaps more importantly, bankruptcy may tie up your book for years. Your publisher, due to financial embarrassment, won't be able to print it, and you, due to this financial embarrassment and its ramifications, won't be able to take it to another publisher. Your tenure case may be deep-sixed along with your publisher's assets.

To protect yourself, press for a clause something like this in your contract:

In the event of bankruptcy, the debtor (publisher) must affirm or reject the author's contract within the terms required by the federal bankruptcy laws. If the debtor chooses to affirm this contract, he or she must also cure any prior defaults.

This means that if the publisher goes under, the publisher has to cancel your contract and return the rights to your book to you, or affirm that your contract is in effect and pay you anything you're owed.

You also might try to protect yourself against the possibility that your publisher will sell off your contract to another publisher with whom neither you nor your tenure committee would want you to be associated. Protect yourself with the following language:

> This contract may not be assigned by either party without the prior written consent of the other. In the event of a sale of all or substantially all of the publisher's assets in the case of bankruptcy, the publisher may reassign this contract; however, before any such assignment, the publisher must pay all and any amounts due and the prospective assignee must agree to perform all publisher obligations.

This clause requires your approval of the new publisher, and requires your old publisher to pay you what you are owed. It also requires your new publisher to assume all the old publisher's obligations to you.

Chapter 15

WAS IT GOOD FOR YOU TOO? DO YOU WANT TO DO IT AGAIN? WITH THE SAME PUBLISHER?

Remarriage is the triumph of hope over experience.
—*Dr. Samuel Johnson*

An option clause in a book contract gives the publisher the right to publish an author's next book. Such a clause may seem like a gift to many authors eager for continued publication, especially academic authors eager for continued publication and eternal tenure. But if you want your present publisher to publish your next book, the option clause won't help you. It binds you, not the publisher. Only very successful authors are given the opportunity to sign contracts that include option clauses binding the publisher as well as the author.

If the match between you and your publisher turns out to have been made in hell rather than heaven, you might want to do some serious thinking about widening your options. And the time to do that is when an option clause first appears in your contract.

The few academic presses that do include such clauses in their contracts rarely insist on them.

"It doesn't make much difference with a university press," B. J. Chandler says. "If you make contact with another press and they're interested, the first press will release you with no hassle at all. I never talked to anyone who had any difficulty about it."

But do you want to sign a witnessed document committing your next work of love and scholarship to a company that may spend the next several years showing you how truly hellish book publishing can be? An option clause, if insisted on, may prevent you from even showing your next book, or your

115

proposal for it, to other publishers, until it has been rejected by your present publisher. One author who signed a contract containing an option clause recalled somewhat ruefully that had he just struck out that clause when the contract was sent to him, the publisher wouldn't have objected.

"It didn't bother me a bit at the time because I didn't think I would write another book and if I did why not let them have first refusal?" says the author, who asked to go unnamed. "I am in fact writing another book in the same field and will in fact give it to my original publisher, but it has occurred to me to write another kind of book for which my original publisher wouldn't be appropriate."

If your publisher resists your attempt to eliminate the option clause altogether, try for the following compromise:

> The author shall be free to submit the proposal for his or her next book-length manuscript to other publishers along with the present publisher. Should another publisher make an offer for the book, the present publisher shall have 14 days to exceed that offer, failing which it shall have no further rights to the manuscript. The author shall remain free to accept or reject the publisher's offer.

This gives you your freedom and your present publisher a fair shot at your next book. An alternative:

> The author agrees to submit the proposal for his or her next book to his or her present publisher before accepting the offer of any other publisher. If, at the end of 30 days, the author and publisher are unable in good faith to agree upon terms, the publisher shall have no further rights to the manuscript or proposal.

Under no condition allow the option clause to stipulate that you must wait until your current book is published before submitting your new manuscript. This could tie your hands for a year or more.

DON'T FIGHT: GRIEVE, ARBITRATE, OR MEDIATE

Blessed are the peacemakers . . .
—The Gospel according to Saint Matthew

Academics tend to be lovers, not fighters. And when they do fight, they tend to be backstabbers, not street brawlers. The long hate is much more common in academia than the quick punch.

Academic writers should be at least as civilized with their publishers. Don't fight: grieve, arbitrate, or mediate.

If you and your publisher can't settle your disagreements informally, your first step should be to file a grievance with the National Writers Union, either its New York headquarters or one of its eleven locals throughout the country. The union's aggressive grievance officers will handle any writer's legitimate complaint without charge as long as that writer is a union member. The NWU uses such weapons as letters, phone calls, and publicity, but will also take your case before arbitrators, or refer you to cut-rate legal services if you decide on court. The union has recovered nearly half a million dollars owed its members since it was founded in 1983.

One NWU beneficiary was Susan Cavin, assistant director of women's studies at Rutgers, who received no royalties for her book because her contract allowed her publisher to subtract many of the expenses of running his company from her royalties even if the expenses weren't directly related to her book.

"I kept asking the publisher for my royalties," Cavin says. "He gave me an accounting of everything he had spent on publicity for my book—every envelope he ever used, every stamp—and concluded that the book had earned $19,000 while he had spent $24,000. That's why he couldn't give me any royalties. I felt he was charging my book for most of the expenses of running his publishing company."

After arguing with her publisher for more than a year, Cavin contacted Philip Mattera, the NWU national book grievance officer, who wrote her publisher several letters and spoke with him on the phone.

"Her publisher wanted to do a new printing and didn't want to ride roughshod over her to do it," Mattera says. "We caught him red-handed."

"He was more responsive to Phil and the union than he had been to me," Cavin adds.

The union and the publisher hammered out a compromise and a new contract, and the publisher sent Cavin her first royalty check, for about $1,600.

If you don't avail yourself of the union's services, you might want to try mediation early on. Mediation is simply the appointing of a third party to informally resolve any disputes between you and your publisher that the two of you haven't been able to resolve on your own.

If mediation doesn't work, the next step should be arbitration: a hearing before a panel that issues a binding and final decision on your dispute.

The alternative to mediation or arbitration is our nation's court system, which undergirds the nation's freedoms and has built many a mansion in the hills of You-Name-the-Town, U.S.A., for the country's trial lawyers. Costs aside, during the years it takes to settle many court cases you could be rejected for tenure at several major universities.

Since most publishers are big and most authors are small, the NWU or mediation is best for the author, with arbitration a close second and the courts a distant third. For the publisher, it may be just the reverse; this is why you should push for a mediation clause in your contract. Publishers rarely agree to mediation, but sometimes do offer arbitration, since if you're really determined you may well cost both of you a great deal of time and money if you go the third route and everybody moves into the courthouse for the duration. Try to have the following language included in your contract:

> Should differences arise under this agreement that cannot be resolved by discussion between author and publisher, the difference shall at the option of either party be submitted to a mutually acceptable mediator. Should this mediator fail to resolve the difference, a panel shall be formed consisting of one representative of the publisher, one representative of the author, and one mutually agreed-upon representative. The decision of this panel shall be final and binding.

The advantage here is that the two of you can pick your own arbitration panel. However, it is more common for publishers to agree to arbitration by a recognized arbitration organization such as the American Arbitration Association. So you might want to try for the following contractual language:

> Any controversy arising out of or in connection with this agreement or any breach thereof shall be settled by a mutually agreed upon arbitrator under the rules of the American Arbitration Association.

Chapter 17

NEVER GIVE UP: PUBLISH WITHOUT PERISHING

Never, never, never, never, never give up.
—The entire text of a commencement speech
delivered by Winston Churchill

Laurence J. Peter was an assistant professor of education at the University of British Columbia in 1964 when he first submitted the manuscript of *The Peter Principle* to McGraw-Hill. The McGraw-Hill editor who rejected the manuscript wrote Peter that "I can foresee no commercial possibilities for such a book and consequently can offer no encouragement." The next 30 publishers to whom Peter sent his manuscript expressed similar views. It wasn't until William Morrow & Company published *The Peter Principle* in 1969 that the book began its life as a best seller and made "the Peter Principle" as much a part of the language as "Murphy's Law" and "Catch-22."

The less well known but indefatigable freelance writer Roland E. Wolseley once sold an article twenty years after it had been repeatedly rejected by many editors.

Stories like this abound among non-academic freelance writers. Of course, these writers, cousins of ours, have a major advantage: their day jobs, whatever other disadvantages they entail, don't require them to publish work a tenure committee will approve, and don't require them to publish during the limited tenure track period.

Solutions? Simultaneous submissions is one. Sending out proposals rather than completed manuscripts is another. (See Chapter 4, Preparing Proposals, for more on both.) Quick revision is another: if your proposal is soundly rejected by all the relevant publishers, emphasize another angle of the subject and send the proposal out again, to a new batch of publishers, as soon as possible. You have no need—and no time—to waste any research and writing you've done. Anyway, why not try to keep hope alive at all times? Life's more fun that way.

Two other solutions: keep two pots boiling, two or more proposals working, at any one time. If the reception given one dwarfs the reception given the other, put all your bets on that one and hope for the best. Or work your book proposals into journal articles.

Time will tell which of your ideas will work in the academic marketplace, and in what format. But never drop an idea until you're sure you've wrung it for all it's worth. As an academic by choice and a writer per force, you have no other option.

Appendix A

NATIONAL WRITERS UNION INFORMATION

*There's nothing to writing. All you do is sit down
and open a vein.*

—*Red Smith*

Whether you're an academic, a journalist, or poet, a fiction, technical, small press, or commercial writer, the stories behind your stories are often harrowing.

- You submit your book manuscript on time and according to specification. Then, without warning or just cause, your publisher declares the manuscript "unsatisfactory" and demands the return of your advance.
- You write two stories for a monthly magazine, but the magazine changes hands and the new owners declare they are not responsible for the obligations of the previous owner.
- You write a manual for a non-profit organization. They subsequently sell it to a commercial publisher and make a profit—but you don't. Your work, they say, was "work for hire" and, anyway, didn't you "do it for the cause?"
- You are seeking tenure at your university and must publish the results of your research. An academic press agrees to publish, but only if you bear the financial risk.
- You write regularly for a big-city weekly. Then you find out that other writers at the publication receive half or—twice—as much as you received for equivalent work. Why the discrepancy? Not even management seems to know.
- You've written an article on a controversial topic. When it appears in the magazine, it contains a conclusion 180 degrees from the one you wrote. And your editor didn't even warn you, much less ask you about the changes.

The National Writers Union is supplying some new endings to these old, old stories.

If you feel isolated in your work or unsure of your rights

If you've ever been badly paid for your work or ill-treated by a publisher

If you believe writers are entitled to equity and fair compensation

You belong in the National Writers Union.

Through collective bargaining and united action, the National Writers Union is giving writers a fighting chance. Only eight years old, the National Writers Union is 3,000 members strong and growing. And we're already making a big, big difference.

- Through ground-breaking collective bargaining agreements covering freelance writers at magazines like *Ms., Mother Jones, Columbia Journalism Review* and *Ploughshares.* Our contracts include rate increases, guaranteed kill fees, prompt notice of acceptance or rejection, and more.

- With new kinds of grievance procedures and aggressive grievance committees that have won more than $500,000 for writers. In Boston, a mass grievance against *New Age* magazine netted $30,000. When Holt, Rinehart & Winston shredded books written by the late Alvah Bessie, a nationwide campaign forced them to pay the replacement value of the destroyed works. In Los Angeles, we pried $100 loose from a magazine that published a member's poem without consent.

- With peer counseling on contracts and agents, a unique agent database and valuable negotiating guidelines. Individual contract counseling has helped hundreds of members negotiate better contracts, even without a collective bargaining agreement. Our database gives you the up-to-date scoop on literary agents. And publications like our *Model Magazine Contract,* and our *Code of Professional Practice for Technical Writing,* and co-published publications such as the one you just finished reading, are creating new rules where there have been none.

- By organizing for change. With efforts like our "fair pay, fair treatment" campaign in the book publishing industry, we're pioneering and developing innovative new ways of representing writers.

- By defending freedom of the press and the First Amendment. Through lobbying, testifying, and mobilizing we've helped beat back attempts to gut the Freedom of Information Act, impose gag rules and censorship, and use the McCarran Act to deport, or deny visas to, foreign writers.

- And by providing unique members-only benefits. Every member now has access to group health insurance and a VISA card and receives our quarterly publication, *American Writer*, as well as local newsletters.

We are a community of writers who care about equity and each other.

In coalition with other artists' groups and unions in this country and abroad, we're building a progressive force for change and working for our rights. By joining the National Writers Union, you can help us and help yourself as we change the power structure of a publishing industry that is large, powerful, and increasingly dominated by multinational conglomerates.

By joining, you can help give a fighting chance to writers everywhere.

National Writers Union, 873 Broadway, Suite 203, New York, NY 10003, 212-254-0279

SAMPLE

Application for Membership

(PLEASE PRINT OR TYPE)

FOR OFFICE USE ONLY		
Date Rec'd _____	Full _____	Computer/$ _____
New/Renew _____	Half _____	Computer DB _____
Local _____	Am't _____	Memb Pkg _____

Name _____

Address _____

City _____

State/Zip _____

Work Phone (___)_____

Home Phone (___)_____

Date _____

QUALIFICATIONS

Membership in the NWU is open to all qualified writers, and no one shall be barred or in any manner prejudiced within the Union on account of race, age, sex, sexual preference, disability, national origin, religion or ideology.

You are eligible for membership if you have published a book, play, three articles, five poems, one short story, or an equivalent amount of newsletter, publicity, technical commerical, government or institutional copy. You are also eligible for membership if you have written an equal amount of unpublished material and you are actively writing and attempting to publish your work.

I meet these qualifications.

(signature) _____

BARGAINING COUNCIL INFORMATION
(check your primary genres)

☐ Journalism
Books
  ☐ Fiction
  ☐ Nonfiction
  ☐ Academic/Text
  ☐ Juvenile
☐ Poetry/Small Press
☐ Technical Writing
☐ Business/Trade Journalism
☐ Insitutional/Nonprofit
☐ P.R./Newsletters
☐ Other: _____

Literary Agent: _____

As an NWU member you are part of those bargaining councils that are negotiating contracts with publishers, publications, and firms for which you have written. Please list all books by title and publisher, plus all newspapers, magazines and firms or institutions for which you have worked as a writer in the past. three years. This information will be kept confidential.

Magazine/Newspaper Title or Book Publisher	Year Last Published

PARTICIPATION

In which local do you belong?
☐ Boston ☐ Chicago ☐ DC ☐ LA ☐ Western Mass.
☐ Minn/St. Paul ☐ NJ ☐ NY ☐ SF
☐ Santa Cruz/Monterey ☐ Westchester ☐ At Large

Your participation is what makes our union strong. Please check those areas in which you can contribute to building the union:

☐ Book organizing
☐ Data Bases
☐ Job Bank
☐ Membership
☐ Grievance handling
☐ Newsletter/PR
☐ Event Planning
☐ Fundraising
☐ Phone work
☐ Mailings/office work

NATIONAL WRITERS UNION DUES

NWU dues are based on your annual income. If your writing income is currently small, but you have other sources of income, we encourage you to pay dues at one of the higher rates. If necessary, you may pay dues in half-year installments (with a slight surcharge for extra handling).

Annual Writing Income	Full Year	Half-Year*
Under $5,000	☐ $60	☐ $35 installment
$5,000-$25,000	☐ $105	☐ $57 installment
Over $25,000	☐ $150	☐ $80 installment

*half-year payments include $5 surcharge

I am making an additional contribution of $ _____

How did you learn about the National Writers Union?

126

Appendix B

LISTBUILDING AREAS OF UNIVERSITY PRESSES

The following listing appeared in the Association of American University Presses 1990-91 Directory. Each press's 1988 new title output is listed in parentheses. The Directory also lists press personnel, phone numbers, mailing addresses, and special series for the American university presses listed below, as well as for the Canadian, international, institutional, and associate members. The annual directory is available from the Association of American University Presses, 584 Broadway, New York, NY 10012.

The University of Alabama Press (38)

History, political science, public administration, Judaic studies, linguistics, southern regional studies, literary criticism, history of American science and technology, anthropology, and archaeology.

University of Arizona Press (36)

Anthropology, space sciences, southwestern Americana, arid-lands studies, natural history, Mexican studies, Native American studies, Asian studies, and creative nonfiction.

The University of Arkansas Press (27)

Biography, short fiction, poetry, translation, literary criticism, history, regional studies, and sociology.

University of California Press (260)

African studies, anthropology, arts and architecture, Asian studies, biological sciences (anatomy, botany, entomology, zoology), classical studies, economics, film and theater, folklore and mythology, geography, history, labor relations, language and linguistics, Latin American studies, literature, medicine, music, natural history and ecology, Near Eastern studies, philosophy, physical sciences (astronomy, chemistry, engineering, mathematics, physics), political science, religious history and interpretation, sociology, urban studies, and women's studies.

Cambridge University Press, American Branch (992 overall)

The humanities, the social sciences, the biological and physical sciences, mathematics, music, psychology, religious studies, reference works, and English as a second language.

The Catholic University of America Press (20)

American and European history (both ecclesiastical and secular), Irish studies, American and European literature, philosophy, political theory, and theology.

The University of Chicago Press (249)

Sociology, anthropology, political science, business and economics, history, English, American and foreign literatures, literary criticism, biological and physical sciences, mathematics, conceptual studies of science, law, philosophy, linguistics, geography and cartography, art history, classics, architecture, education, psychiatry, psychology, and musicology.

Columbia University Press (152)

Reference, history, philosophy, American, English and foreign literatures, Asian studies, film studies, women's studies, journalism, music, art, archaeology, anthropology, social work, sociology, political science, political economy, international affairs, business and economics, law, psychology, life sciences, geology, geophysics, astronomy and space science, evolutionary studies, and computer science.

Cornell University Press (147)

Anthropology, Asian studies, classics, history, literary criticism and theory, nature study, philosophy, political science, veterinary science, and women's studies.

Duke University Press (63)

The humanities, the social sciences and related science subjects, with lists in American and English literature and criticism, American and European history, American studies, political science, Soviet and East European studies, Latin American studies, economic history, theory and development, environment/resources and energy, political philosophy, ethics and religion, music and dance, photography, state and local government, urban and regional planning.

University Presses of Florida (34)

S.E. archaeology, international affairs, contemporary South America, the Caribbean, the Middle East and Africa, Southern history and culture, native Americans, folklore, postmodern literary criticism, philosophy, women's studies, ethnicity, natural history, humanities, medieval studies and poetry.

Fordham University Press (24)

Principally in the humanities and the social sciences.

Georgetown University Press (16)

Languages and linguistics (especially Romance linguistics), ethics studies and theology.

University of Georgia Press (60)

American and English literature, southern literature, U.S. and European history, medieval and Renaissance studies, eighteenth-century studies, folklore, American studies, women's studies, civil rights, African-American studies, critical theory and film, photography, anthropology, natural history, and regional trade titles.

Harvard University Press (107)

The humanities, the social and behavioral sciences, the natural sciences, and medicine.

University of Hawaii Press (48)

Asian and Pacific studies in history, art, anthropology, economics, sociology, philosophy, languages and linguistics, literature, political science, and the physical and natural sciences.

The Howard University Press (4)

Afro-American and African studies, the humanities, visual arts, history, literature, sociology, anthropology, and psychology.

University of Illinois Press (110)

American history, American literature (especially twentieth-century), American music, Black history, sport history, religious studies, communications, cinema studies, law and society, regional photography and art, philosophy, architectural history, environmental studies, social sciences, western history, women's studies, working-class history, short fiction, and poetry.

Indiana University Press (127)

African studies, anthropology, archaeology, Asian studies, Arab and Islamic studies, art, Black studies, business, cultural and literary theory, environment and ecology, film, folklore, history, Jewish studies, linguistics, literary criticism, medical ethics, Middle East studies, military studies, music, philanthropy, philosophy, politics and international relations, public policy, religious studies, science, semiotics, Soviet and East European studies, state and regional studies, translations (especially Russian and Chinese), Victorian studies, and women's studies.

University of Iowa Press (30)

Literary criticism and history, short fiction, American history, regional studies, poetry, early music, archaeology and anthropology, natural sciences, Victorian studies, history of photography, aviation history, biography, and autobiography.

The Iowa State University Press (88)

Aviation, agriculture, journalism, design, engineering, home economics, education, sciences and humanities, veterinary medicine, and regional history.

The Johns Hopkins University Press (123)

American and European history, Caribbean studies, classics, earth and planetary sciences, economics and economic development, environmental studies, geography, health policy administration, history of technology, science and medicine, international relations and security, literary theory and criticism, medicine and public health, natural history, psychology and human development, regional books of general interest, and U.S. government and public administration.

University Press of Kansas (33)

American history, women's studies, presidential studies, social and political philosophy, political science and public policy, military history, environmental studies, sociology, and Kansas, the Great Plains, and the Midwest.

The Kent State University Press (18)

American cultural, military, diplomatic, and Civil War history, art history, women's history, medieval studies, Ohio regional studies, American and British literature and criticism, science fiction and utopian studies, music studies, and North American (particularly Midwestern) archaeology.

The University Press of Kentucky (40)

American and European history, military history, American, English, and Romance literature and criticism, political science, international studies, folklore and material culture, women's studies, anthropology, Afro-American studies, sociology, and Kentucky, the Ohio Valley, the Appalachians, and the South.

Louisiana State University Press (66)

The humanities and the social sciences with special emphasis on southern history and literature, southern studies, French studies, Latin American studies, political science, poetry, fiction, and music (especially jazz).

The University of Massachusetts Press (35)

American studies and history, black and ethnic studies, women's studies, cultural criticism, architecture and environmental design, literary criticism, philosophy, poetry, political science, sociology, and books of regional interest.

The MIT Press (169)

Architecture, design arts, photography, economics and finance, information-computation-cognition, computer science and artificial intelligence, cognitive science, neuroscience, materials science, formal linguistics, aesthetics and art criticism, critical theory, continental philosophy, history and philosophy of science, general science (astronomy, biology, mathematics, physics), ecology, and environmental sciences.

The University of Michigan Press (45)

Literature, classics, history, theatre, women's studies, political science, anthropology, economics, archaeology, regional trade titles, and textbooks in English as a second language.

University of Minnesota Press (44)

Literary and cultural theory, American culture, feminist studies, biology and the earth sciences, personality assessment, clinical psychology, psychiatry, health sciences, philosophy, Nordic area studies, Upper Midwest studies.

University Press of Mississippi (29)

American literature, American history, American culture, southern studies, Afro-American studies, women's studies, American studies, social sciences, popular culture, folklife, art and architecture, natural sciences, references, and other liberal arts.

University of Missouri Press (29)

American and European history, American, British, and Latin American literary criticism, political philosophy, art and art history, regional studies, poetry, and short fiction.

Naval Institute Press (61)

Naval biography, naval history, oceanography, navigation, military law, naval science textbooks, sea power, shipbuilding, professional guides, nautical arts and lore, and technical guides.

University of Nebraska Press (92)

English literature, American literature, translation, political science, music, the American West, the Great Plains, the American Indian, food production and distribution, agriculture, natural history, psychology, modern history of western Europe, and Latin American studies.

University of Nevada Press (12)

History, biography, anthropology, and natural history of Nevada and the West, Basque peoples of Europe and the Americas.

University Press of New England (35)

American and European history, literature and literary criticism, cultural theory, art history, philosophy, psychology, education, books of regional interest, and natural sciences.

University of New Mexico Press (63)

Social and cultural anthropology, archaeology, American frontier history, western American literature, Latin American history, history of photography, art and photography, and important aspects of the Southwest and Rocky Mountain states including natural history and land-grant studies.

New York University Press (91)

Economics, women's studies, history, politics, psychology and psychiatry, sociology, New York City and State regional affairs, literature and literary criticism, Middle East Studies, and Judaica.

The University of North Carolina Press (70)

American and European history, American and English literature, American studies, southern studies, political science, sociology, folklore, religious studies, legal history, classics, women's studies, music, rural studies, urban studies, public policy, Latin American studies, anthropology, business and economic history, health care, regional trade books, and North Carolinia.

Northeastern University Press (18)

American history, literature and literary criticism, American studies, poetry, criminal justice, women's studies, music, and books of regional interest.

Northern Illinois University Press (16)

American history, European history, Russian history, Latin American history, political science, British literature, and American literature and regional studies.

Northwestern University Press (25)

Literary criticism and theory, philosophy, theatre studies, drama, Eastern European literature, Renaissance studies, media criticism, South American literature, African literature, Chinese literature, Russian literature, Jewish studies, political science, poetry, and classical studies.

University of Notre Dame Press (46)

Philosophy, ethics, sociology, political science, history, theology, medieval studies, liberal arts, law, and business.

Ohio University Press (50)

Nineteenth-century British literature and literary criticism, history, nineteenth and twentieth-century continental philosophy, health sciences, African studies, and Western Americana.

Ohio State University Press (20)

Afro-American studies, computer and information science, criminology, early modern European history, human development, international women's studies, modern literature and literary theory, philosophy and cognitive studies, political science, regional studies, sports history, U.S. history, urban studies, Victorian studies, fiction, poetry, and belles lettres.

University of Oklahoma Press (66)

Regional studies, western U.S. history, American Indian studies, classical studies, language and literature, natural history and political science, energy studies, women's studies, art and archaeology.

Oxford University Press, American Branch (1,588 overall)

Scholarly monographs, general nonfiction, Bibles, college textbooks, medical books, music, reference books, journals and children's books.

University of Pennsylvania Press (62)

American and British history, anthropology, art, architecture, biological sciences, business, computer science, economics, folklore, history of science and technology and medicine, law, linguistics, literature, medicine, music theory, women's studies, and regional studies.

The Pennsylvania State University Press (35)

Art and history, literature, philosophy, religious studies, Latin American studies, criminology, geography, law, international relations, political theory and comparative politics, U.S. politics, sociology, American and European history and science, technology and society studies.

University of Pittsburgh Press (37)

The humanities, the social sciences, and community medicine, (especially mental health).

Princeton University Press (156)

American, Asian, European, Latin American, Middle Eastern, Russian, and Eastern European history, archaeology, classics, art history, architecture, film, music, philosophy, literature, religious studies, astrophysics, biology, chemistry, computer science, engineering, geology, history of science and medicine, mathematics, ornithology, physics, anthropology (especially European), demography, economics, constitutional and international law, political science, sociology (especially historical).

Rutgers University Press (60)

Literary criticism, film, art history and criticism, American history, women's studies, anthropology, sociology, geography, life and health sciences, history of science and technology, and regional studies.

University of South Carolina Press (46)

Rhetoric and speech communication, religious studies, international relations, contemporary literature, southern history and culture, military history, maritime history, international business, industrial relations, physical education, marine science.

Southern Illinois University Press (52)

American and English literature, philosophy, speech and rhetoric, First Amendment studies, journalism, education, sociology, political science, archaeology, anthropology, linguistics, botany, and zoology.

Southern Methodist University Press (9)

American studies, anthropology and archaeology, composition and rhetoric, ethics and human values, fiction, film and theatre, regional fiction and nonfiction, religious studies.

Stanford University Press (81)

The humanities, the social sciences, and the natural sciences and law with particular emphasis in anthropology, health policy, history, literary criticism and theory, linguistics, political science, psychology, sociology, systematic botany and zoology, women's studies, and studies involving China, Japan, Latin America, and Russia.

State University of New York Press (123)

Philosophy, religion, Middle East studies, Jewish studies, Asian studies, work and labor studies, women, linguistics, and education.

Syracuse University Press (37)

Contemporary Middle East, international affairs, Irish studies, Medieval and Renaissance studies, especially the role of women, New York State and the region, Iroquois studies, American history, special education, environmental management studies, peace studies, and conflict resolution.

Teachers College Press (35)

Scholarly, professional, text, and trade books on education and related areas.

Temple University Press (67)

American studies and history, sociology, political science, health care, women's studies, comparative policy, philosophy, photography, ethics, social theory, work, sexuality, political economy, urban studies, Black and ethnic studies, educational policy, Philadelphia regional studies, and anthropology.

The University of Tennessee Press (28)

American studies, African-American studies, history, religion, anthropology, folklore, vernacular architecture and material culture, literature, women's studies, Native American studies, Southeast studies, Caribbean studies, and Appalachian studies.

University of Texas Press (60)

The humanities, the social sciences, and the natural and physical

137

sciences, regional studies, translations of Latin American literature, photography, classics, architecture, film, American studies, Eastern European studies, Latin American studies, Mexican American studies, and Middle Eastern studies.

Texas A&M University Press (30)

Texas and the Southwest, American and western history, natural history, the environment, military history, economics, business, architecture, art, and veterinary medicine.

Texas Tech University Press (16)

Anthropology, biological sciences, engineering, the environment and conservation, folklore, translations, earth science, museum science, regional studies, classical studies, history, literary criticism and theory, poetry, and fiction.

University of Utah Press (25)

Anthropology, western history, regional studies, Mormon studies, Mesoamerican studies, Middle East studies, philosophy and ethics, poetry, and fiction.

The University Press of Virginia (47)

U.S. Colonial history, literary criticism, bibliography, women's studies, architectural history, American decorative arts, and regional titles.

University of Washington Press (88)

Anthropology, Asian-American studies, Asian studies, arts, aviation history, forest history, marine sciences, music, regional and general art history, history and culture of the northwest, native American studies, Scandinavian studies.

Wayne State University Press (66)

African-American studies, Judaica, classics, folklore, literary criticism and theory, film and television studies, urban and labor studies, health sciences, regional and local history, ethnic studies, and speech pathology.

University of Wisconsin Press (52)

General scholarly titles.

Yale University Press (188)

The humanities, the social and behavioral sciences, and the natural sciences.

INDEX

141

143

144

44   36